This Might Work

A Collection of How-Tos

Robin Peter Zander

Opening Remarks

Since 2023, I've written Snafu, a weekly newsletter about influence and persuasion. But every so often – instead of an article about non-sales selling – I write a tactical how-to on a subject I've recently attempted: how to fast, or how to train a dog, or how to buy a used car.

I enjoy writing these articles because they become references for me when I need to remember how to do that specific skill.

I sat down recently and compiled the best of these how-to guides. I hope you enjoy!

Writing With AI

I have typed every word in this book.

I'm fascinated – and terrified – by the potential of AI. But I write because I love the process of writing – how difficult it is and how it forces me to think.

I use AI every day. In my writing, I use AI to point out flaws in my thinking and grammatical errors. But every word in this book is my own.

Disclaimers

Copyright © 2026 by Robin Peter Zander

All rights reserved. No part of this publication may be reproduced, distributed, or transmitted in any form or by any means, including photocopying, recording, or other electronic or mechanical methods, without the prior written permission of the publisher, except in the case of brief quotations embodied in critical reviews and certain other noncommercial uses permitted by copyright law.

Medical & Health Disclaimer

The information provided in this book is designed to provide helpful information on the subjects discussed. Prior to attempting any activity discussed in this book, consult with your physician. This book is not meant to be used, nor should it be used, to diagnose or treat any medical condition. For diagnosis or treatment of any medical problem, consult your own physician. The publisher and author are not responsible for any specific health needs that may require medical supervision and are not liable for any damages or negative consequences from any treatment, action, application or preparation, to any person reading or following the information in this book.

TABLE OF CONTENTS

1. HABITS

HOW TO START WRITING 2
HOW TO BUILD A CREATIVE HABIT 8
HOW TO RUN A SELF-EXPERIMENT 12
HOW TO CREATE THE CONDITIONS FOR LEARNING 16
HOW TO STOP UNWANTED BEHAVIORS 23
HOW TO BE DISCIPLINED 29
HOW TO FAST 35
HOW TO MAINTAIN FLEXIBLE GOALS 44

2. LEARNING

HOW TO RAISE A PUPPY 50
HOW TO BUY A USED CAR 58
HOW TO BUY A HOUSE 70
HOW TO GO DOWN A RABBIT HOLE 85
HOW TO CLIMB A MOUNTAIN 89
HOW TO TILT AT WINDMILLS 94

3. SALES & STORIES

HOW TO SELL 100

HOW TO TELL A GREAT STORY 105

HOW TO GET STARTED IN SALES 110

HOW TO GET LEADS 115

HOW TO MAKE COLD CALLS 121

HOW TO SELL ACCOUNTING 126

HOW TO SELL VIDEO 133

HOW PIXAR TELLS STORIES 142

4. WORK

HOW TO OVERCOME RESISTANCE 146

HOW TO BE PERSISTENT 151

HOW TO RAISE MONEY 156

HOW TO CONDUCT AN INTERVIEW 163

HOW TO HIRE OFFSHORE 168

5. EVENTS

HOW TO RUN AN UNCONFERENCE 176

HOW TO RUN AN UNUSUAL EVENT 182

HOW TO CURATE A CONFERENCE 188

6. CHAOS

HOW TO FAIL BETTER	194
HOW TO TRAIN FOR CHAOS	198
HOW TO SURVIVE AI	200
HOW I'M SURVIVING THE NEXT 4 YEARS	205

7. EMOTIONS

HOW TO STOP FEELING OVERWHELMED	212
HOW TO FEEL BETTER	216
HOW TO USE FEAR AS A GUIDE	221
HOW TO DEAL WITH PAIN	227
HOW TO GRIEVE	231

8. RELATIONSHIPS

HOW TO DATE	238
HOW TO ASK FOR WHAT YOU WANT	250
HOW TO SET BOUNDARIES	255
HOW TO HELP PEOPLE DO WHAT THEY WANT	258
HOW TO TRAVEL WITH FAMILY	263
HOW TO CHANGE SOMEONE YOU LOVE	268

1

HABITS

HOW TO START WRITING

Originally published September 2023

When my friend Karen X Cheng launched her startup, GiveIt100, she invited me to teach all the steps necessary to learn to do a handstand. She also suggested that I turn my expertise into a short book.

In 2014, I self-published a book called How to Do a Handstand, which – due more to the timing than the quality of my writing – sold thousands of copies and became a best-seller in Japan! I fell in love with writing and the mental clarity that comes from articulating and refining my ideas.

A few years later, based on Responsive.org and my annual Responsive Conference, I self-published my second book

Responsive: What It Takes to Create a Thriving Organization. Unfortunately, that was also the same year that I sold Robin's Cafe, went through a difficult breakup, and burned out. I stopped writing altogether.

In 2023, in an effort to get back into writing, I launched my newsletter. In the last five months, I have published more than in the preceding five years. Today, I'll share why writing is a valuable skill to practice, how to start writing, and how to overcome Writer's Block.

Why I Write

Writing Clarifies Thinking

There are a lot of ways to improve your thinking – meditation, rhetoric, and others. But writing is one of the best methods I know. The process of articulating an idea, and then revisiting and honing it, results in clearer thinking.

Get To Know Your Ideas

When I sit down to write, I often don't know what I'm going to say in advance. Through writing, I discover beliefs and opinions that I didn't know I hold. The discipline of writing forces me to express an idea, then test and refine it.

The Editing Process

I write a lot of words that never get published – and that's the point. Just like a professional athlete will practice their sport thousands of times for every competition, the most important part of writing is the process of revising and editing. We get better with practice.

Practice With Practice

I seek out skills that reinforce my ability to learn. Conducting interviews teaches you to ask better questions. Surfing teaches you to relax and not fight the power of the ocean. Writing trains you to think clearly. Pursue disciplines that train you to be better outside of that discipline.

Test Your Ideas

Publishing your writing creates stakes – even if the consequences are low. I have to reckon with typos and flaws in my thinking. When I share an idea, other people engage with it, which allows me to evaluate my idea further.

There's No Such Thing As Writer's Block

I have on my desk a water flask given to me by the bestselling author and marketer, Seth Godin, that says, "No such thing as writer's block."

What we call writer's block is the internal state where your self-judgment and fear of failure supersedes the desire to write. We ascribe the term writer's block to this sensation and then disclaim the responsibility for our feelings. Identify that self-judgment, and then begin.

How To Start Writing

Start Small

When I set out to write this newsletter, I set myself the task of writing for a handful of minutes each day. My goal was to send a 500 word email to a few friends once a week. Today, I'm averaging 2 hours a day, have published more than 200,000 words, and I'm planning my next book. But my aspirational goal still remains small. My goal is to write 1,000 words each day – quality be damned. Set your baseline for success as low as possible. When you make your objective so small that success is almost inevitable, you're more likely to build a new writing habit.

Practice Every Day

Inertia is hard to overcome when starting from zero. It's easier to continue with what you've already been doing than to start from nothing. Even if one or two days go by where I don't write, I find it more difficult to get into the groove of creating than if I maintain a daily practice. However small your writing habit, strive to do some little bit of writing every day.

Writing Is A Discipline

As a former professional athlete, I work out every day – whether I want to or not. By contrast, I've always waited for inspiration to strike before sitting down to write. Treat creativity as a discipline; something that you return to every day, whether you feel like it or not. Judge your progress by whether you showed up that day, not by how much work you got done.

The Importance Of Setting

In *The War of Art*, Steven Pressfield describes a variety of good luck charms that he has on his desk. When I first read Steven's book, I dismissed the need to have everything in place before sitting down to write, but in the last few months I've come to recognize the importance of setting.

As we say in restaurants, "mise en place" or everything in its place. When I write in the same location every day, have a cup of tea in hand, and have my Timebirds Timer running, it is easier to get into a creative groove.

Write And Edit Separately

Writing and editing are different stages of the creative process. Both are important; good writing requires each. When I look back on the struggles that I had writing Responsive, they are due to attempting to edit and write the book at the same time. First, create your messy first draft. Then, edit and critique your work.

I wish that I had kept writing after publishing my last book *Responsive*. But as the saying goes, "The best time to plant a tree was ten years ago. The second best time is today."

HOW TO BUILD A CREATIVE HABIT

*Originally published
July 2023*

The Artist's Job

My mother is a professional artist. She has been making art, paintings, and mezzotints, for more than 40 years. Every day, for my entire life, I've watched my mother get up, go out to her studio, and paint. That's her work: to put brush to canvas and create.

But when I compare my own creative habits to the clockwork regularity of my mother's practice, I realize that I'll go to great lengths to avoid my own creative work.

- A painter paints.
- A writer writes.
- An entrepreneur builds a business.

That's the job.

Start Small

I've been intending to write regularly since I published *Responsive: What It Takes To Create a Thriving Organization*. But I've been avoiding writing because writing is really hard work.

Creating feels risky, my inner critic is loud, and a new project can be hard to fit into my already busy days. To combat this, I started small, tiny, even writing just a few minutes every day to build up my confidence.

The process of creating, whether a cafe, YouTube channel, or new musical instrument, begins by putting one foot in front of the other. Start smaller than you currently think possible. As an old teacher of mine used to say: "Decrease your ambition."

Trust you will eventually grow your tiny habit, but don't set yourself up for failure by setting the bar too high. Make your creative habit so small that today's success feels almost inevitable.

Manage The Inner Critic

One reason you aren't starting might be as Ira Glass explains, that you have taste. Having a strong aesthetic sense or creative vision is great. But don't let your taste stop you from getting started. High standards make for a mean inner critic and you censor yourself before you even begin.

If you have something that you want to express, but you aren't sure how to convey it, don't let perfection hold you back from starting. The best way to overcome the inner critic is just to begin.

What Feels Good After?

When something is hard, that's a sign that it might be worth doing.

I've been moving every day for 20 years, and there are still days that I don't want to exercise. I never get up in the morning eager to get into my 39-degree cold plunge.

Fasting for 5 days is as difficult a project as I've ever undertaken.

I don't do these things because they feel good in the moment. I do them because I feel great after I'm done.

Habits, even uncomfortable ones, are an investment in your future. The feel-good results aren't always immediate, but remembering those results will come is one way to motivate yourself to get started.

HOW TO RUN A SELF-EXPERIMENT

Originally published on November 2024

I first heard the term "self-experimentation" as an undergraduate in behavioral psychology.

My professor gave a few examples of his own. He went a month with no sugar, which made carrots taste unbearably sweet. He tried sleeping with his head lower than his feet, which felt miserable and his wife refused to continue. There were many more.

I think he would have enjoyed teaching an entire seminar about self-experimentation, but he only introduced the concept, and we were left to explore for ourselves.

Which I did.

First in athletics, but then across diet, romance, work, and every other domain of my life, I've run thousands of self-experiments.

In 2023, I went more than a week without food. In 2024, I ate just three ingredients for five months. I sit in 38-degree water for several minutes every morning. All from an insatiable desire to answer the question, "What if...?"

In work – and throughout our lives – experiments can feel like big endeavors. To lose fat, you need to Diet with a capital D. Gaining muscle is assumed to be hard and with a side of suffering. (I put on 15 pounds of muscle while eating exclusively bison, zucchini and quinoa earlier this year.)

In our workplaces, experiments are even harder: As an employee, you might get fired. As a boss, I might get sued.

Experimentation requires enough space to try something new. You have to be able to consider whether this experiment is worth trying, evaluate the potential outcomes, and survive the impact.

But the truth about running an experiment – whether self-experimenting with diet or implementing a new process at work – has huge potential upside.

Start Small

Every time I think I've fully grokked this idea, I find new dimensions of "starting small."

Popularized by BJ Fogg and discussed in his book *Tiny Habits: The Small Changes That Change Everything*, the smaller you can make an experiment, the easier it is to try. Progress comes through small steps that eventually create dramatic change.

As Buckminster Fuller said, "There is nothing in a caterpillar that tells you it's going to be a butterfly."

Make It Reversible

In physical movement, there's a concept of "reversibility." A well-executed roll in Brazilian jiu-jitsu can be paused midway through and reversed. All non-dynamic movement can be assessed for quality by whether it can be reversed at any time.

Whenever we changed the menu at Robin's Cafe, doing so created new challenges for my employees who had to learn the new recipes. But a new menu that is rolled out can also be rolled back, and I could talk to each employee in advance to see how they feel about the new concepts.

In running experiments, ask yourself "Is this reversible?"

Measure Impact Over the Long Term

When trying a new diet or implementing a new process, it is natural to want to see change immediately.

But lasting change doesn't happen overnight. It happens over weeks, months, and years.

The quicker something is to implement, the more likely it is to flip back to its previous homeostatic state. The longer the period, the more you're likely to see lasting change.

Measure in decades, not in days.

What Did You Learn?

Throughout each experiment, ask yourself "What did I learn?"

When experiments fail – like the first and fiftieth time I tried to give up sugar – this is a question that kept me going. And when you are making progress, this is a way to celebrate and expedite progress.

I always want to remain capable of change and reinvention. In business, I aspire to build a learning organization that can equally adapt to our rapidly changing world.

To succeed in the world today, you need to be able to constantly reinvent yourself and your work. That starts with the question, "What did I learn?"

HOW TO CREATE THE CONDITIONS FOR LEARNING

Originally published September 2023

In the fall of 2003 I broke my neck on a trampoline. (That sounds dramatic – I know – but it actually isn't uncommon in gymnastics). To heal, I began to study with a woman who specialized in working with kids with autism.

While her work focused on helping parents help their special needs children, I found it also helped me with my injury. Pretty soon, I too began working with autistic kids and traveling around the world to teach parents how to help their children flourish. In the process, I became a student of how different variables create a supportive learning environment for these children and families.

Even more than the rest of us, kids with autism respond to their environment – to the emotions of the people around them and the situations they are in. They don't respond to pressure.

Learning is a vulnerable process that requires that we try new and uncomfortable things. But just like any other skill, you can get better at learning with practice. Today I want to share how to create an ideal learning environment. While most of us don't require ideal conditions for learning, these tools are applicable everywhere.

Attention

Pay Attention To What Is Happening While It Is Going On

I found that kids' attention was the deciding factor in their ability to learn. What we attend to, we make bigger. This idea is the bedrock for learning.

We live in a world where everyone – and everything – is vying for our time and attention. Advertisements, social media, push notifications all interrupt our focus for their own agendas.

Practice channeling your attention – whether for a few minutes or a few hours. Direct your attention to the things you are most interested in improving. The more concentrated attention you can bring, the faster you'll be able to learn.

Slow

"Slow Is Smooth And Smooth Is Fast"

Moshe Feldenkrais, founder of the somatic discipline the Feldenkrais Method, said, "Fast, we can only do what we already know."

Learning demands that we stretch outside our comfort zones, and that is much harder under pressure, urgency, or force. Learning benefits from spaciousness and safety.

While it is counter-intuitive in today's fast-moving world, slowing down is the best way to get faster. A similar idea comes from the Navy SEALs: "Slow is Smooth and Smooth is Fast." Moving slowly means moving with intention and attention; it reduces the risk of making the kinds of mistakes that then would take more time to undo and correct.

Consider how you'd approach a skittish horse or a nervous child. The best way isn't with force or aggression, it's instead to approach gently and from the side. To move your hand slowly towards the horse's muzzle or ask the child, in a quiet tone, how their day has gone.

In slowing down you are better able to absorb and make sense of novel information. You'll create better conditions for learning, and deeper integration.

Variation

Playing With The Variety Of Options Available

When I was in university, I studied the impacts of variable practice. Here's how it works:

You and I are on a basketball court, taking turns shooting hoops. You shoot from the free throw line while I shoot from all over the court. In effect, you are learning to shoot free throws – and only free throws – while I'm learning to shoot baskets.

Assuming we are starting from a similar baseline, your free throws will outperform mine during this practice period. You are shooting from a single location while I am shooting from all over, so you get more practice at the specific task.

But when we test at the end of the trial period – even as little as 30 minutes later – I have better performance. My performance is still better several days later, and from a variety of conditions around the court. Practicing with variation results in more learning.

This concept extends beyond the basketball court. When you are feeling stuck, try variations around the edges of what you can currently do to learn more thoroughly. Approaching the problem from a different angle offers the opportunity for more connections and perspectives.

Enthusiasm

Enjoy The Process

During the years I worked with autistic kids, I often attended training programs for parents of special needs children.

One day at a workshop, I walked into the dining hall to see my friend Stan in the center of a circle of attentive parents. As I walked up, Stan paused what he was talking about and asked: "Robin, why did you come up?" I responded that I was curious about what was going on.

Stan explained that he was being enthusiastic deliberately, so that the parents in the room would be excited to learn from him. He went on to share that this was what each of us needed to do to create the conditions for success and learning for the children in our lives.

It worked: when I was engaged, excited, and energetic, the kids I worked with were more engaged with me and our shared activities.

Even when you aren't trying to teach or inspire someone else, you can be deliberately enthusiastic about what you're learning. Excitement reinforces positive feelings about the process, which, as I've discussed in this essay about celebration, is a great way to incentivize behavior change.

Flexible Goals

Be Flexible In How You Define "Success," Especially During The Learning Process

Goals are great. They give you direction and motivation. But your goals need to be reevaluated regularly because every step you take provides more information about whether that goal is realistic or even worth your effort.

Most often, you are learning something new with a clear objective in mind. I worked with kids with autism to help them function more effectively. You practice shooting basketball with the goal of making baskets. We practice for the outcomes that practice gets us.

But if the metric of success is too narrow, it sets us up for a win/lose binary. Instead, working towards a goal is ultimately about practicing the skill of learning.

Growth is a vulnerable process. Take the pressure off and you're better able to absorb new information!

I've long since recovered from my trampoline injury, and the years of working with autistic kids are also behind me. But when I'm feeling stuck or not learning as fast as I want, I incorporate more enthusiasm, flexible goals or variation into my daily practice. I invite you to do the same.

HOW TO STOP UNWANTED BEHAVIORS

*Originally published
July 2023*

I have always enjoyed training dogs. Dog training is about reinforcing good habits, both for the dogs and in ourselves. And I've found there is a lot to learn about habits – and ourselves – from the process.

I was working with a dog recently; he is 100 pounds, and a complete love. Unfortunately, he had some traumatic experiences as a puppy and can be reactive. But this was the first time he was reactive with me: teeth bared, snapping. He alternately wanted my attention and was scared that I might hurt him.

In all fairness, he had just been to the vet and had to be sedated. The next day, still recovering, he snapped at me and wouldn't let me pet him, like he usually does. I had a moment of despair: I sure as hell don't want to interact with a reactive dog! But also, up until this incident, I'd thought of this dog as a friend. And I began thinking about how likely it is that a dog can ever be completely trained out of unwanted behaviors.

How completely – how thoroughly – can behavior really change? As I was considering this dog, I realized that changing behavior is like riding a bicycle.

When I first learned to ride a bike, I fell off hundreds of times. But in the thousands of hours I've logged since, I can count the number of tumbles I've taken on one hand – even though I race down city streets at 45 miles an hour.

But accidents do happen. We do sometimes make mistakes or revert to unwanted behaviors.

It can be tempting to avoid making mistakes by removing the conditions that led to them or ceasing the activity altogether. A way to ensure I never fall off my bike again would be to never get on it in the first place. I could take the same approach with this dog. He and I could never interact, or he could stay locked in his house alone. But these aren't viable solutions. All are based on fear, perfectionism, and a fixed mindset.

We all have unwanted behaviors and habits we want to change. But, that's not really how learning works. Put anyone in a stressful enough situation and they can revert back to earlier patterns. I eat a lot of mint ice cream, and would like to change this behavior. Offer me mint ice cream when I'm hungry and

I'll probably eat it. Put me on my bike, on a bad road, amidst distracted drivers, and I may get into an accident.

Even if we never, for the rest of our lives, repeat a habit we're trying to extinguish, we always have the capacity to do so.

What this means is that, instead of looking for perfection, the solution is to look for learning. When I repeat a habit I want to avoid – when this dog snaps at me when he's scared, when I eat too much ice cream, or when I fall off my bicycle – there's only one option: get back up and try again.

Build From Where You Are

Building from where you are is usually the best option, since it adds on to what we already do and increases the range of what's possible. With this dog, that means first acknowledging that he's reactive today, and not letting my ego get in the way. Staying frustrated, or even feeling betrayed ("We were friends yesterday!") clouds judgment. Working with where he is today means not denying the reactive state he's in, which in turn allows me to avoid repeating interactions that will reinforce the undesirable behaviors.

Don't Try To Remove Unwanted Behaviors

I have some counterintuitive advice: don't try to remove unwanted behaviors. You may want to remove unwanted behaviors, but it is rarely that simple. Habits and behaviors can't simply be turned off; that's not how neuro-plasticity works. Change comes by rewiring the brain and building upon what is currently possible. We crowd out undesirable behaviors by positively reinforcing desirable ones. Focus on the behaviors you want to encourage and the habits you want to cultivate.

Reinforce What You Want

In interacting with a reactive dog, I want calm and gentle behavior towards me, other people, and other animals. My goal, then, is to positively reinforce the dog every time he offers me, or anyone else, the slightest bit of gentleness. Getting him to focus on treats and positive interactions is a much stronger incentive than yelling at him (and thus scaring him further).

Work Around The Edges

Instead of trying to repress unwanted behaviors, work around the edges of what is currently available. Take what is currently easy and try small variations. With the dog, that might mean that petting is off the table at first, and I have to begin training with a bit more distance than I'm used to. With my current addiction to mint ice cream that might be:

- Trying a different flavor of ice cream (to get me out of my habitual rut).
- Eating out of a bowl (because then I'll demolish the whole pint).
- Drinking water before I have ice cream (I've learned that I sometimes reach for ice cream when I'm thirsty).
- Making a fruit smoothie instead of ice cream (it comes close to the temperature and texture that I'm seeking).

Progress Isn't Linear

One moment of reactivity isn't indicative of how an interaction is going to go tomorrow. When I eat too much ice cream, it often feels like I'm repeating a "bad" habit and failing to practice a "good" one. But a moment of failure is just that: one moment. The real mistake is to consider one misstep a mark of complete failure. In times of stress we revert back to more primitive versions of ourselves. For me, that might be stress eating ice cream as a form of self-soothing. For a dog, that can mean protecting himself the best way he knows how.

Learning happens like a ball repeatedly rolling down a hill of sand. With every iteration, the grooves of the ball's path become deeper and deeper and increase the ball's tendency to follow a similar pattern. That doesn't mean that the ball will sometimes roll along a different route, but the more a pattern is reinforced, the more consistent that habit will be.

My consumption of mint ice cream is something I'm working on. I eat more ice cream when I'm stressed, hungry, and it is readily available. But I've begun iterating on habits to change my relationship and these habits.

I've never trained a reactive dog before and I'm nervous! But I know that change is not only possible, but – given the right prompts, patterning, and reinforcement – it is almost inevitable.

Behavior change, however minor or significant, is the culmination of millions of small influences, moments, and habits. Regression isn't necessarily going backwards. Recalling that, I've got nothing but excitement for all of the behavior change ahead.

HOW TO BE DISCIPLINED

Originally published September 2024

A few weeks ago, someone told me I was the most disciplined person she knows. That feedback was disconcerting because, growing up, I was often told that I lacked discipline. And I guess I never updated my self-image.

I have never been good at forcing myself to do things that I don't want to do, which is how I'd always defined discipline.

Discipline Isn't Hard

Over time, I've come to see this definition as nonsensical. The things I'm told require discipline are things that I want to do.

- I want to exercise every day.

- I want to get into the cold plunge every day.
- I fast regularly.

But I only ever do things that I want to do.

It has taken a while, but I've come to the conclusion that when most people say "discipline" they mean consistently doing things that appear hard to them.

People are stunned when I share that I ate just three ingredients for 5 months. (The first question is "What were the three ingredients?" Answer: bison, zucchini, and quinoa. The second is "Didn't you get tired of the same meal?" Oddly, no.)

Once I decided, very clearly, that I was going to eat that minimalist diet, I wasn't tempted by ice cream or peanut butter.

Nothing is particularly hard when I've decided that I want to attempt it. Hard things are only hard when we are conflicted or not sure we're ready to commit.

Take Personal Responsibility

Discipline is lauded, but the idea isn't well defined. Ownership – taking personal responsibility – is a better way to discuss the same idea.

Each of us is only doing what we want to do at any time. The path forward towards anything – great health, wealth, relationships, or just sitting in very cold water – requires recognizing what we want, knowing why, and then taking baby steps towards that desired outcome.

Getting Started Is The Hardest Part

Doing difficult things isn't hard. Getting started doing difficult things is.

I'll procrastinate for hours getting into my cold plunge. By comparison, the difference between 1 second and 30 seconds sitting in frigid water is easy.

Now that I've recognized this resistance in my cold plunge routine, I'm looking for that same procrastination and avoidance elsewhere.

Discipline And Disciple Share The Same Root

I was discussing the idea of discipline with colleague Marie Szuts recently, when she casually pointed out that "discipline" shares the same root as "disciple."

Discipline originates from the Latin word "discipulus" which means student or learner.

When we remove the more modern punitive quality of the word, we're left with discipline as something closer to the word "practice."

The 51% Philosophy Of Behavior

A lot of people I know subscribe to a theory of percentages of behavior.

A friend of mine will say that he both wants to do something and doesn't. If 51% of him wants to do something, thus he does it.

It's convenient to say that I both want to do something and don't want to do something. But it is also inaccurate!

I can only do something or not do something.

I either get into the cold plunge or I do not.
I either eat that pint of ice cream or I do not.
A continuum of behavior doesn't exist.

Personal Responsibility

We don't have good language to describe personal responsibility.

There's no good language – at least in English – to describe that state where I don't want to get in the cold plunge, but I've decided that I'm going to do so, thus I actually do want to, so I go ahead and get in anyway.

That's what we're talking about. Taking personal responsibility for our behavior and our actions.

What Am I Avoiding?

Currently, I'm noticing what I'm avoiding.

Just like I avoid getting in the cold plunge in the morning, the mark of success is not just whether I get in but how quickly I do so. Am I avoiding this behavior?

Try This

When I have kids I don't want to teach them about discipline in the way it was drilled into me. Instead I want them to feel good for having done hard things.

- A runner's high after a 5-mile run.
- The feeling of your brain having been stretched after writing an essay.
- When you sit and read a book that challenges you to think differently.

My homework, then, is to do something that you "don't want to do" and to do it with attention.

- Go for a walk and notice how difficult it is.
- Take a cold shower, instead of a hot one.

I can't prescribe something "difficult" for you because it depends on your baseline. (A cold shower isn't hard for me anymore, even though a cold plunge is.)

The key is to notice how you feel before you engage in this behavior. Notice your temptation to avoid that behavior, and then how you feel afterwards.

HOW TO FAST

Originally published November 2024

A friend of mine is embarking on his first 4-day water-only fast, so I sent him a voice memo with all of my lessons learned from fasting over the last few years. Then, I realized it'd be useful to write this up.

First, my bonafides.

In 2024, I didn't eat for a total of 46 days. I did those fasts in 1 to 6 day increments throughout the year – and learned a lot in the process.

This is an article about how to do a long term fast, not about why you should. But first I'll articulate a few of the benefits I've found.

Caveats: I'm not a doctor and don't play one on the Internet. This isn't medical advice. Please consult with your medical provider. And please don't sue me.

Why I Fast

Autophagy

Autophagy is the state in the body where the body recycles cells. This happens during any fast – even just not eating for twelve hours overnight results in mild autophagy.

We're built this way – to break down the most unhealthy cells in the body so that healthy cells predominate and to decrease the chance of them turning into cancer or causing other harm.

Cancer Prevention

I first came to learn about fasting because my best friend, having been diagnosed with breast cancer, was doing multiple water fasts every month.

By creating a context in the body inhospitable to cancer cells, the theory – and a great deal of evidence – suggests you decrease the chance of cancer growing or metastasizing.

It is, of course, a much longer conversation, but three books I recommend about cancer are:

- *The Emperor of All Maladies: A Biography of Cancer*
- *Cancer as a Metabolic Disease*
- *The Cancer Resolution?: Cancer reinterpreted through another lens*

The absolute maximum that most bodies can sustain is not eating one day for every two days of eating. I wouldn't recommend even that much for anyone not combating cancer.

A Caffeine Reset

I'm a lifelong caffeine drinker.

I love nothing more than green tea or pu-erh first thing in the morning. (I also love coffee, but gave it up when I sold Robin's Cafe.)

I've tried many times over the years, to cut caffeine entirely, and suffered caffeine headaches and even nausea.

During a 5 day water-only fast – during which I don't drink anything but water – not only don't I suffer caffeine withdrawal, but I come through the experience feeling as if I haven't had my regular green tea or coffee for many months.

Fasting provides a great reset.

Our Bodies Are Made To Fast

I don't believe much about "paleo" or the paleolithic diet, but I do think it is useful to consider how our ancient ancestors ate. And it is abundantly clear that humans did not have food as readily available as we do today.

Our bodies, it turns out, are built to be able to fast. Physically, we can do a couple of days without food without adverse effects. (Psychologically, of course, is another matter.)

If we can fast with ease, it makes intuitive sense to me that there might be some benefits to doing so every so often.

Get Comfortable With Heightened Adrenaline

The psychology of fasting is difficult. And managing the heightened adrenaline that comes with a fasted state is my least favorite element.

After the first day or two, the body kicks into a state of heightened energy and lethargy. You're either on or off!

But intense adrenaline, which most of us don't experience outside of extreme experiences like competition or a car crash, is also a useful state to get familiar with.

Getting comfortable with high adrenaline is good practice for when the world gives you something really worth freaking out about.

Reevaluate Your Relationship With Food

I love food! And to my detriment, I've been known to eat, for flavor, even when I'm not hungry.

The most useful element of fasting I've discovered is the forcing function of having to re-evaluate my relationship with food.

Practice being hungry, wanting to eat, and not eating. Being hungry, wanting food, and not eating. The definition of delayed gratification.

Tactics For Fasting

Electrolytes

The worst moments during my longer fasts have come from not having enough water and electrolytes.

"Drink plenty of water" is the most common advice articles and YouTube videos give. And it is true: during a long fast, you have to drink more water than during your normal life.

Because you aren't absorbing any liquid through food and to get into a fasted state, the body dumps a lot of water, it is really important to stay hydrated. But the advice of "drink water" falls flat when I'm pumping full of adrenaline, have a splitting headache, am cold, and – in short – feel miserable.

The secret – in addition to drinking water before you feel like that – is consuming enough electrolytes.

The advice I was given is to eat pinches of salt through my fast. That's terrible advice. Salt on the tongue isn't great at the best of times, but when you haven't tasted flavor for days, straight salt is the last thing I'd recommend.

Similarly, LMNT, while a useful tool, is much too strongly flavored and contains Stevia, both of which interfere with a fast. Chock full of sugar, you absolutely must avoid Gatorade. Anything with sugar negates a fast, and consumed during a fast can result in refeeding syndrome, which is quite serious.

My preferred form of fasting supplement is Trace Minerals tablets. While they aren't small, and a serving size is 6(!), you can take these with just a sip of water, down a lot in a short period, and they contain the sodium, magnesium, potassium, and trace minerals you need for a complete electrolyte balance.

Random aside: I've always struggled with high altitude acclimatization, which is unfortunate because I love climbing big mountains. Taking these Trace Mineral supplements has, in recent years, completely eliminated my challenges with acclimatization.

Start And End With Keto

This is a little hack that I have only discovered recently and that I wish I had known prior to my earliest and most difficult fasting.

"Keto," or the ketogenic diet is, essentially, a modified fast. The body enters autophagy and burns fat for fuel like during a deeper water-only fast.

"Keto flu" is a term ascribed to the state of discomfort, and sometimes even nausea, that sometimes accompanies entering ketosis if you are unaccustomed to keto. It is much easier to deal with the symptoms of keto flu before entering a full fast with its heightened adrenaline, sleep deprivation, and other challenges.

Like fasting, the body gets accustomed to ketosis. With practice, you can enter ketosis more readily and more gently over time. When you begin a longer fast with a few days of eating a keto diet, you short circuit that challenged state by entering it prior to fuller demands of a full fast.

Start With 24 Hours

As with most things worth doing, start small.

My friend is considering a four day fast, never having done even as much as 24 hours previously. That's going to be difficult because there is a lot to learn about your own body through the process of fasting.

Instead, start small. Fast for 24 hours before trying 36 hours, 48 hours, or longer.

During a 24 hour fast you won't enter a state of deep ketosis, but you will get a sense of your relationship with food and hunger. For me it was a revelation that you can go to bed hungry and wake up the following morning feeling just fine.

I did my first 24 hour fast in early 2023, and by the end of the year had done multiple 5 and 6 day fasts.

Start small. Your gains will compound.

Beware The Witching Hour

I call the hours of 6 and 9 pm each evening the witching hour. This is the period during which the human body is most able to put on calories and retain weight.

If we trace the time back to prehistory, this is when humans were most likely to eat large meals and then be able to rest, so our bodies have learned that this is the time to signal hunger, and also to store calories.

This is the most difficult time during a fast.

In the morning, I wake up – and while I might miss my caffeine rituals – generally feel fine.

During the day, there are short bouts of hunger, but if I keep busy – it helps to focus on relatively unimportant tasks – they are easily passed by.

But in the evening my body is ready to eat. This is the time that I don't allow myself into the kitchen or around other people eating food. Sitting with someone at breakfast? No problem. But joining someone for dinner is a miserable experience.

The best advice I have to get through the witching hours is to distract yourself. (I suggest "Chef" and other movies depicting food.)

Go to bed early. Find something that you can do to make that time pass.

Conclusion

If all of this sounds difficult, it is.

Long term water-only fasting is probably the most difficult thing I do on a regular basis. (My current cadence is two 5-6 days fasts each year.)

But, like most difficult things, it is among the most rewarding.

Not only have I re-evaluated my relationship to food (among other things, cutting out sugar and alcohol from my diet), but the knowledge that I can delay gratification and take small steps into doing something that previously was impossible gives me the confidence to attempt future hard things.

I hope this is useful, and inspires you to try something new and difficult.

Start small, listen to yourself, and as ever, let me know if you ever need anything.

HOW TO MAINTAIN FLEXIBLE GOALS

Originally published October 2025

The night before Day 2 of Responsive Conference 2025, I spent an hour agonizing over how enthusiastic everyone was. I was worried the conference hadn't struck the right balance of existential dread and optimism for the future – given that I feel a fair bit of existential dread myself!

But after stressing over my attendees' experience for an hour, I looked back at the agenda I'd curated for Day 2 – starting with my old boss Vivienne Ming and ending with Eldra Jackson III – and realized that the program I'd created would provide attendees the experience I wanted them to have: real, raw, but not pessimistic.

One of the things I like most about live events – whether as an MC, speaker, or athlete – is that once the show begins, we have to let go of the outcome. As much as we've practiced our lines, rehearsed our talks, or trained in advance, once the performance begins, there's nothing to do but continue.

One of my early teachers, Feldenkrais-disciple Anat Baniel, described this idea as "flexible goals." In the subsequent eight years I spent working with autistic kids, maintaining flexible goals was the only path forward! A myopic focus on hypothetical outcomes, like "I want my child to be neurotypical," impedes progress.

Maintaining flexible goals – or letting go of the outcome – doesn't mean that you don't have an outcome in mind.

When I am trying to sell tickets to Responsive Conference or a client on behalf of Zander Media, I want them to buy! But that's only one of a handful of goals I hold simultaneously – including to be of service. Maybe there is someone I can introduce, a book I can recommend, or something else that would make a difference in their lives.

Let Go Of The Outcome

Anytime I find myself feeling urgency or anxiety, I remind myself "Let go of the outcome."

In the case of my attendees' experience of Responsive Conference Day 2, the solution was simple. I'd already curated an excellent experience that didn't shy away from difficult topics. From our opening and closing keynotes to topics ranging from AI to politics to the Safari animals who joined us at lunch, the experience of Day 2 provided my attendees with a rich and varied experience.

I'd already done the hundreds of hours of preparation necessary. All I had to do was let them enjoy the experience.

Letting go of the outcome is an emotional act. It is more about coming up with a half dozen ways in which other outcomes – in addition to your goal – could be just as good.

In the case of Responsive Conference 2025, if my attendees have too good an experience, is that a bad thing? So, they feel optimistic leaving the conference – and only afterwards are confronted by the realities of our rapidly changing world. There's nothing wrong with providing a bit of escapism.

But if I'm trying to sell something specific or my mortgage depends on a certain level of earnings, it can be difficult to stay flexible. I deliberately make a list of alternative outcomes:

- If someone doesn't buy from me, they're looking out for their best interests.
- Maybe I haven't done enough preparation? Maybe I'm not telling a compelling story?
- Or perhaps what I'm selling doesn't fill a pre-existing need.

In the months leading up to Responsive Conference 2025, one reminder I had to give myself was to "Be less entitled."

As salespeople, we are not entitled to someone else's attention – not to mention their money! If I was asking for help from colleagues to promote the conference, it was my responsibility to make it easy for them to promote. And when someone bought a ticket, take a moment to celebrate that small victory – instead of immediately calculating how much farther I still had to go.

Try This

What are you trying to accomplish? List out 5 alternatives, beyond your primary objective.

Even with your primary objective in mind, can you make one of these secondary goals as big or bigger than the first? Can you want more for the person you're talking to than for yourself?

It helps to write out the goals, and then write an explanation for each.

2

LEARNING

HOW TO RAISE A PUPPY

Originally published on February 2025

A friend of mine just got an 8 week puppy! I've raised two dogs from puppyhood, and helped a dozen other people do the same. This is what I've learned.

Expect Interrupted Sleep

Interrupted sleep comes with the territory. I often suggest raising a puppy to people who are considering having a child. It's good practice.

As with a human baby, a puppy needs whatever it needs right now! Whether that's to be let out in the middle of the night to pee or just your comfort and attention because your puppy has never slept apart from its litter, expect weeks – or months – of interrupted sleep.

Torn Slippers Are Your Fault

Some bad news: when your puppy pees in the house or tears up your slippers – that's your fault.

A young dog doesn't know that the house isn't somewhere to pee. Like a young human child, a puppy doesn't have bladder control. Similarly, an anxious or a teething dog wants to chew. It is up to you to give it something to chew on.

It is important to remember that your puppy isn't doing something wrong. It is just following its natural proclivities. It is your job to monitor your puppy.

Don't get angry when your dog makes "mistakes."

Crate Training

If I could teach every new dog owner one skill it would be crate training.

The first rule of crate training is never to use the crate as punishment. Encourage your dog into the crate. Make it cozy. Make it home. Think of the crate as the spot the dog returns to when it is tired, wants to rest, or wants to be alone.

A crate has the additional benefit of being a closed container, so your puppy can't escape and peer and chew your slippers upon waking.

Training Cadence

To raise a young dog, develop a training cadence:

- When your puppy first wakes up, take them out of the crate and outside to potty.
- Then, offer your puppy some water and food.
- Then play with your puppy until it is tired.
- Take your dog outside to potty, again.
- Then, put it back in the crate for a nap.

This is going to be your cadence for the first few months!

Positive Reinforcement

You know those metal spiked collars that people use to try and control their dogs? Don't do that. They are cruel and they hurt.

A lot of early animal behavior management was done with dolphins. And it turns out that you can't force a dolphin to do something it doesn't want to do. Want a dolphin to take food from your hand? Jump out of the water to impress spectators? Be kind to that dolphin or it'll just swim away.

The same is true for puppies. (And, I believe, for humans. But that's an argument beyond the scope of this article!)

I believe that you should train your dog exclusively through positive reinforcement.

Negative Reinforcement

Let's take a mild counterexample. Let's say your puppy pees on the carpet – which is a minor offense. Your puppy didn't pee on the carpet to upset you. It just needs to pee!

Even if you catch your dog in the act, your aggressive "No!" is more likely to scare your dog than inform it that this behavior is undesirable. Your puppy doesn't yet know how to control its bladder. And by shouting "Bad dog!" you are creating a disconnect between you and the animal.

It is also hard to catch your dog in the action. It is more likely that scolding will come after the incident and your dog won't even make the connection between peeing and your displeasure. All they will know is that you're unhappy.

Focus on reinforcing the behaviors you do want, and the behaviors you don't will extinguish themselves.

Reinforcement Words

In the 1960s, dolphin trainer Karen Pryor began using a clicker to train her dolphins at Sea Life Park in Hawaii. Based on B.F. Skinner's operant conditioning, using a clicker (literally a device which makes a loud clicking sound) allows trainers to mark desired behaviors at a distance before delivering a reward. Pryor popularized clicker training through her book *Don't Shoot the Dog!*, which is a foundational text in the field of positive reinforcement training. Another way of doing the same thing is using a reinforcement word to mark behaviors you want to encourage.

Pro Tip: Don't Use "Yes"

A lot of dog trainers will recommend using the word "Yes!" as a reinforcer, since most people don't constantly have a clicker near to hand. I've come to regret using that word.

Instead, pick a word – perhaps even in a different language – that you don't use every day, or else your dog will get confused when you use the word as a part of everyday speech.

Your Dog Is A Reflection Of Your Nervous System

There's a quote I've heard Tim Ferriss say that his dog is a reflection of his nervous system.

This might not be true of everyone's dog, but for my border collie, Riley, it is certainly the case.

When I'm stressed, Riley is anxious. And when I'm chill, Riley is likely asleep. I can always tell how I'm feeling just by looking at my dog!

Every dog is a reflection of their owner. And the more you are aware of your own emotions, the better you'll know – and train – your dog.

Know Their Motivations

Some dogs are food motivated and some aren't. Some want to be pet and lauded, and others want a job to do. Just like people, a dog's motivations are its own. You can do a good job training your dog only after you know what motivates them.

Know Your Breed's Tendencies

Some generalizations:

- Labradors want attention, praise and food
- Herding dogs need a job
- Bully breeds want to keep their people safe

If you are lucky, your dog will be food motivated. That makes everything much easier because food is a very simple, concrete reinforcer of behavior. Praise, while a little more nebulous, is also something that many dogs respond to. Understand your breed's tendencies and temperament. Plan accordingly.

Say "Come" Only When You're Sure They Will

Most of us misuse the word "Come" with our dogs. Too often, we use it in moments of impatience when we don't want to be troubled to traipse outside through wet grass to get them.

When you should shout "Come!" – knowing full well that your dog would rather keep playing with another dog, smelling interesting smells, or eating something it shouldn't – you are reinforcing that your dog doesn't need to do what it is told. We are what we repeatedly do. So are our dogs!

Use the recall word "Come" only when you are 100% certain your dog will come when called. Otherwise, go and get them.

Puppies Are Rude

This phrase always surprises new dog owners. But puppies lack the social graces of adult dogs, who know when other dogs want to be approached and when they don't.

Adult dogs may set boundaries with a growl or a harmless snap at an over-eager puppy. This is appropriate!

You can always tell the impact of an adult dog and a puppy's encounter by whether the puppy cowers in fear or immediately comes back for more.

You're The One Who Needs To Change

We believe that dog training is about changing the behavior of the dog. Actually, it's the opposite. Dog training is an opportunity to get to know yourself – and for you to change so that you can become a good steward of your animal.

Your dog is just being itself. If your puppy pees on the floor, it is because you didn't take it outside in time. If it chews a shoe, you should have given it more opportunity to chew appropriate toys, and shouldn't have left your dog unattended. Every dog behaves according to its instincts.

You are the one who needs to adapt, and only by doing so will you be able to train your dog.

HOW TO BUY A USED CAR

Originally published January 2025

I have two friends looking to buy used cars right now. Over the last fifteen years, I've purchased six used cars and resold five of them.

While I'm a novice compared to car salesmen, I have more experience with used cars than the average person, and thought it would be useful to share what I've learned.

Assumptions

I don't have "fuck you" money. If you do, none of this matters.

I went for a hike in Marin County last week, and jogged by a house with a $275,000 Bentley, and two $350,000 supercars in the driveway!

This article isn't for the owners of that house. They don't buy used cars.

I prefer to save $10,000 by buying a used car.

I want something safe and reliable with zero drama.

My primary goal in getting a new car is that it is safe, reliable, and drama-free.

My 2016 Toyota Prius isn't sexy. But it is clean – inside and out – the leather seats have heaters, and the same model saved my life in 2022.

I don't want another car soon.

This article is written with the assumption that you don't want to buy a brand new car every two years.

I don't expect to upgrade my car for at least another 5 years. I'd rather spend some time now to save time over the next decade on repairs or another purchase.

This won't be the last car I ever drive.

This isn't the last car I'm going to own.

I hope to eventually own a used-but-nice sports car just for the fun of it!

My current car isn't that.

I don't mind doing a little bit of leg work – i.e. don't buy the first car you come across.

I'm an entrepreneur, but you don't have to be. I do anticipate that anyone benefiting from this article is willing to do just a little bit of leg work.

If you would rather spend an extra $10,000 or $20,000 – great! Buy your car new from a dealership. But three extra hours now (including the ten minutes it'll take you to read this article) will save you thousands of dollars over the next few months.

Buy A Used Car

I've never purchased a brand new car.

You save between 15-20% of the price of a car when you don't buy a car from a new car dealer. A $40,000 car will lose $6,000-$8,000 in value in the first year.

By year 5, that shiny new car is worth less than 50% of its original price.

I buy makes and models that have stood the test of time and cars that are 3-5 years old. My ideal car has been made for more than a decade, is about 5 years old, and has as few miles on it as I can find.

Talk to Mechanics About The Type of Car to Purchase

I like talking to mechanics. They're busy, terse, and usually covered in grease. But if you can get one talking, you'll learn everything you need to know.

I used to drive a 2007 Subaru Forester. Every time I brought the car in for an oil change, my mechanic commented that this car – which I drove past 175,000 miles – was bulletproof.

(That Subaru Forester, which we nicknamed "Indy," was totaled in an accident when someone hit me on the freeway. Yet another great car that saved my life.)

I asked my mechanic what car he would recommend if I were ever to upgrade, and he pointed me to a late model Toyota Prius – which is what I drive today.

Sexism And Cars

When I was 21, I dated a woman who was 16 years older than me. Early on, I picked her up at the airport in my 1994 Honda Civic Hatchback. When she rolled down her window, the glass fell out of the door frame.

I was mortified, but she quickly and efficiently opened up the door, put the glass back in, and then put everything back together. Later that summer, she and her father rebuilt my little Civic's suspension.

That ex-girlfriend, and many women, know more about cars than I ever will. But the world of cars is sexist. If you are buying a car, and aren't a man yourself, bring a man with you. You'll be treated with more respect and get better deals than a woman purchasing on her own. Sad, but true.

Get A Third Party Inspection

If there was one tactic I could impart to everyone purchasing a car it would be this: get the car inspected before you buy.

One of the most overlooked things that any mechanic can do for you is conduct a "third-party pre-purchase inspection."

After you have researched, sourced a car that you are interested in, looked over it in person, and taken it for a test drive, take your car to a nearby mechanic and have them do a pre-purchase inspection.

Source the mechanic in advance and call them to ensure they're willing and available to do an inspection. It'll cost you $150 and take a couple of hours.

Any trustworthy seller will have no problem with you paying a mechanic to do a brief inspection. If your seller objects, walk away!

When I was buying my current 2016 Toyota Prius, I found a local garage with no affiliation to my seller, scheduled, and then brought in the Prius. I paid $120 and the inspection took one hour.

As I'd suspected, the car, which had 35,000 miles on it, was pristine inside and out – except for one thing.

The tires were bald.

I was able to negotiate the price of new tires off of the purchase price of the car and saved myself $1500.

A third-party inspection will tell you everything you need to know about your car.

Low Miles

Get a car with low miles. This, alongside a mechanic's inspection, is the surest way of determining the longevity of your vehicle.

Get a used car in the make and model that you want with as few miles as you can afford.

A car with low miles is one of the surest ways to determine that it will serve you well for years to come.

Safety

In 2022 I was in a significant car crash. My Prius was hit by an SUV on the freeway going 70 and both cars were totaled. I was lucky to walk away with my life.

Do your research. Just Google or type into ChatGPT: "How safe is a [whatever make and model car you are considering]?"

The Toyota Prius is known to be reliable and safe. When my insurance paid out, I purchased the exact same make and model of car again.

One additional tip that I learned when I used to ride motorcycles (known as "donor bikes" in Emergency Rooms around the world) is that the color of your vehicle impacts whether it will be seen on the road. A white or light colored car is more visible than a red, black or dark colored car.

If you can, buy a light colored car.

Know Your Details – Make, Model, and Era

Know the make and model of the car you want.

After my 2022 car crash, I wanted another Toyota Prius.

But I also know about the generations of the Prius. The first and second generation Prius had problems with their batteries, which got solved in the third and fourth generation.

If I was buying a Prius today, I'd go with the fifth generation because they've changed the body shape and it is less unattractive.

Do enough research to know the quirks and foibles of the make, model and generation of the car you want.

Knowing what you want makes finding it easier.

Don't Buy A Lemon

In 2012, I bought a manual transmission Subaru Impreza. The car was great in the snow, sporty enough to feel sexy, and a joy to drive.

But had I talked to a mechanic in advance, I would have learned that that era Impreza was notorious for transmission problems. And sure enough, six months later, the transmission seized up.

I bought the car for $5000 and had to sell it for parts for $1500. An expensive lesson!

A "lemon" is the term ascribed to cars that are notoriously problematic.

Research the make, model and era of your car. Talk to a mechanic who works with those cars, specifically, and ask about potential problems.

Do Your Research

Advertisements vs. In Real Life

Advertisements are a bad indicator of how good something ultimately is in real life. The only things I pay attention to in an ad when I'm buying a car are:

Is it the Make, Model and Year you want?

Are there pictures?

How many miles?

Clean title (Don't buy a Salvage title)

Is it within a distance you're willing to travel?

Everything else comes out when you and your mechanic inspect the car in person.

Private Owner vs. Used Dealer

I don't have a strong preference between buying from a private owner and a used car dealer, but it is worth knowing which you're dealing with in advance.

A private seller is just someone like you and me who has a car to sell. They'll know more about this specific car than you do, but otherwise they're just a random person.

A used car dealer is a different thing entirely. By default, I don't trust car salesmen. I'm sure there are great car dealers in the world, but most car salesmen are pushy – it is how they are taught.

They are in the business of selling cars, and their job is to sell you a car in as little time as possible.

They'll know all the tricks: how to make a car look and smell great, how to negotiate, how to play on your insecurities.

Just like when you are talking to lawyers or doctors, apply the "Bring a Friend" rule. When buying a used car from a dealer, always bring a friend.

Lean on your friend for support, and don't get rushed into anything. Never buy from a used car dealer on your first visit.

You Don't Have To Be An Expert To Trust Your Eyes

Ten years ago, I was hired as the first employee for a non-profit educational technology company.

My boss Vivienne Ming tasked me with hiring software engineers. I'm not an engineer and had never hired software engineers before!

It turns out, you don't have to be technical to make good technical hires if the people you are hiring are willing to tolerate enough questions.

In the same vein, you don't have to be an expert on cars in order to ask enough questions about this specific car, its background, and the owner's driving habits that you can learn everything you need to know.

My advice, as usual, is "Ask more questions!"

Always Negotiate

I was fortunate to spend a lot of my youth in the large open air markets of Latin America. I learned from a very young age that price is always negotiable.

We assume that the price listed on an item in the grocery store or at a coffee shop is what must be paid. That is never true with cars.

When you are buying a used car, the price is open for negotiation. Come prepared to negotiate or bring someone with you who is.

Be Willing to Walk Away

The final piece of advice for buying a used car – or anything else for that matter – is don't fall in love until after you have finalized the purchase.

When you are negotiating something as significant as the price of a car, it helps to be as dispassionate as possible.

Remember that there are many more like it available in the world. Likely, there are thousands of this specific car available over the next few months. Don't be in a rush.

The person in any negotiation who is willing to walk away will get the better deal. Be willing to walk away (even if you plan to come back later), and you'll do well buying your car.

HOW TO BUY A HOUSE

Originally published September 2025

Last month, I bought a house.

Buying a house is more complicated than nearly anything else I've done – besides, perhaps, running a business. Over the course of the eight months leading up to the purchase, I learned a lot. So today I'm sharing the article I wish I'd been able to read when I started.

This is not an argument for or against buying a house. If you want to be talked out of buying a house, read Ramit Sethi. If you want to hear reasons to buy a house, ask a Boomer. Instead, this is what I wish I'd known about house buying when we got started back in February.

I've worked in a lot of industries, including many dysfunctional ones:

- I've worked in large non-profit arts organizations.
- I've worked within family-owned small businesses.
- I had a chef throw a plate at my head as a server in a restaurant.
- I've worked in fast-paced, drama-filled tech companies.
- I've obtained a myriad of impossible-to-get permits at Robin's Cafe.

I've never encountered as backward, corrupt, and intentionally complicated an industry as real estate!

Let's define some terms.

People You'll Meet

Buyer – That's you!

Seller – The current owner of a property.

Agent – Agents work for either the seller or the buyer – but actually they work for themselves. Their goal is to get you to buy or sell a house, and serve as a liaison between you (the buyer), the seller's agent, and the seller. Agents aren't financially motivated to help you get the best deal because their commission is a percentage of the price of your house. A small price reduction barely affects their fee, even though it matters a lot to you. You are not legally required to have an agent in most states.

Mortgage Broker – These folks help find your mortgage – assuming you aren't paying all cash. They're very salesy and eventually sell your mortgage to someone else. The benefit is that they're available all hours and can get you information very quickly. The alternative is working directly with a single mortgage banker. I suggest avoiding mortgage brokers altogether and talking to a local Credit Union.

Companies You'll Work With

Real Estate Brokerage – Agents work within brokerages, and split income, usually 50/50, with their brokerage. Real estate agents also list houses for sale through their brokerage. There are small, boutique brokerages and also national chains like Compass and Coldwell Banker.

Mortgage Company – The company that holds your mortgage. If you get a mortgage with a specific bank or credit union, they're not likely to sell your mortgage to a third party.

Title Company – The company that ensures successful transfer of ownership between the buyer and seller.

Terms You'll Hear

Buyer's Agent vs. Listing Agent – Typically, a Buyer and Seller each have an agent, and agents discourage you from communicating directly with the other party because it keeps them as the middleman.

Pre-approval vs. Pre-qualification – These are terms you'll hear from your mortgage broker, and represent whether you are qualified for a mortgage. Pre-qual is a soft estimate of how much you'll be able to borrow. Pre-approval is documented and stronger.

Foreclosure – When a bank is selling the property, instead of a person. A lot of the usual laws don't apply, so this is not for the faint of heart.

In Contract – An agreement between buyer and seller that the buyer will purchase the real estate, assuming specific conditions are met.

Earnest Money – Money you put down (usually 3%) to show proof that you are serious about buying a specific property.

Contingencies – The requirements that need to be met before you buy.

How It Started

Our adventure started in February of 2025. My then-girlfriend and I were planning on renting, when – seemingly out of the blue – she texted me a house for sale. One house we saw that weekend – a dilapidated mansion with spectacular views – became the focus for my learning for the next five months.

The mansion had a lot going for it – great views, extremely quiet, an abundance of indoor and outdoor space, pool, garden, easy rental opportunities, and more.

It was also a completely ridiculous project! It had been a party house – built in the 1970s and then illegally rebuilt – which we later learned triggered county requirements like seismic retrofitting and a sprinkler system.

There were three levels of decks with incredible views, but they had been poorly built and were on the verge of collapsing. We discovered two nests of bees in the walls – so active in the spring that the buzzing could be heard inside the house!

After five months of research and seven offers on the property, we walked away.

More than the repair and reconstruction required, we walked away because of the county requirements. The onus on a new owner to make up for the previous decades of illegal construction was too high.

We bought another house in the same city, which also has views, a pool, and rental opportunities. Our new house isn't a mansion, and needs only modest repairs – and we're very happy. But I learned more about real estate during this months-long sprint than I ever thought possible.

Here are some of my takeaways.

Mindset

Don't Fall In Love Until After You Buy

It's really helpful if you don't fall in love with a single property until after you own it. This is the single biggest purchase most people will ever make. The decision to buy is usually made emotionally.

Instead, try not to get too excited – until after you've purchased. Obviously, you don't want regret. Make sure you like the house you're preparing to buy! But too often people fall in love and then get into a bidding war out of the desire to win a deal.

An Entrepreneur's Mindset

The thing that helped me the most through my real estate learning journey was what I'll call an "entrepreneur's mindset."

We wanted a home, yes. But I also didn't want to lose money on a project – if anything, I wanted to make money. Know how to protect your downside and plan for contingencies in case things go wrong.

If your circumstances change and you can no longer afford your mortgage, what are you going to do? What are the ways this property could cash flow, even if you weren't living in it? Are there cosmetic repairs you could make that would improve the value of your home?

They Treat You Like The Product, But Actually You Hold The Power

I'm fascinated by how different industries talk about their customers. At Robin's Cafe, we had diners. At Zander Media, we have clients. At Responsive Conference, we have attendees. Facebook, OpenAI and most software companies have "users" – which is the same term that drug dealers use to describe their customers.

In real estate, agents call property "inventory" and us – their clients – are called "buyers."

There's a sense as you begin to get serious about a property that you are a cog in the machine. Agents will push you to bid on a specific property saying "this is only an initial bid." Mortgage brokers request that you sign documents before you're ready.

The most important thing to remember is that you hold all the power. As the buyer, you can walk away at any time. (Though if you wait too long and contingencies are past, you stand the risk of losing your earnest money.)

You always have the power to walk away.

Research

Know What You Want

My then-girlfriend and I had lots of criteria starting out:

- We wanted a house that was not too far from San Francisco
- That was safe
- And that we could afford
- We wanted to be within walking distance from an interesting town
- Ideally we wanted open space nearby
- The house should have rental opportunities
- And best case scenario for it to have a pool
- Weirdly, we both had a thing for double front doors – just because that felt fancy

However big or small, list the criteria you want in a house. You'll have to settle on some of them, but the clearer you can be on what you want, the more likely you are to get it.

See A Lot Of Houses

The best way to learn about houses is to see lots of houses.

Agents are great for this – but don't commit to working with one agent for a long time, or maybe ever. You can call the listing agent – the person who is showing the house – and ask to see it.

I prefer not going to Open Houses because there are other people and a (false) sense of urgency. Even driving by houses for sale is useful to get a sense of regions and neighborhoods.

Do Your Research

In this industry more than anything else I've ever experienced, it's essential to do the research.

The more thoroughly you get to know a specific region, neighborhood, and even a specific street, before you decide which house to buy, the better off you'll be.

Use ChatGPT to do Deep Research on a variety of topics related to things you see in each house you visit. Ask real estate agents a lot of questions. Talk to people on the street.

Get Lots Of (Free) Quotes

I'm surprised that home buyers don't visit homes they are seriously considering with an entourage of contractors, plumbers and electricians.

There are two different types of quotes — those you pay for and those you don't. If you call a local HVAC company and request a pre-sale quote, they'll charge you. Instead, if you say that you are planning to buy this house and just want to plan for your future, they'll likely come to the house, look around, and send you an estimate of costs for free.

A lot of the difference depends on whether they write up a multi-page summary of their findings or just a single page with a price. Either works fine when it comes to negotiating down the price of the house.

Even if you did have to pay for every technician at every house you're considering, those few hundred dollars would save you tens of thousands in having avoided bad decisions.

Talk To The City Or County

One of the most under-leveraged aspects of real estate is talking to your local jurisdiction — the city or county within which your property falls.

Even just the question "What's this city/county like to work with?," which any agent or contractor should be able to answer, will help inform your decision about the amount of work you're willing to tackle and the amount of bureaucracy you are willing to wade through.

The county where the mansion sits is quite a bit easier to work with than the city within which we now reside. But since our new house requires so much less renovation, we decided that trade-off was worth it.

Talk to your local jurisdiction before you buy!

Read The Fine Print

I'm continually shocked that most people don't read every bit of fine print in every document. The very first real estate agent who showed us a house asked that I sign an exclusive agreement with him even in order for him to show us the property. Had I not read the contract in advance, we would have been stuck with him without recourse.

The title company who transferred ownership of our new house from the previous owner to us was surprised that I requested the 250 pages of legal documentation in advance of the day of signing. And then surprised again that we protested that they had only given us one hour to review the documents in person.

Reading fine print and intentionally obscure legal language is difficult. And, as you go into a hundreds of thousands of dollars project, it is also absolutely necessary.

Never, ever sign without reading all of the fine print.

Cautions

Everyone Has Something to Teach You

Real estate, especially when you're just starting out, is a matter of talking to a thousand people. Everybody has something to teach you.

In the last seven months, I've been on the roof of ten properties with at least a dozen different roofers. Every time I go up, I learn something new about roofs from a casual comment the roofer makes.

Talking to an abundance of people – even if you only learn one new thing from each – will enable you to make better decisions going forward.

A False Sense of Urgency

As with most forms of unethical selling, everyone will try to create a false sense of urgency. Agents will tell you to bid now. Mortgage bankers will tell you you have to sign today, or else deadlines won't be met.

And it is true, especially in a competitive real estate market, that timing does matter. But it rarely matters as much as people will have you believe.

Don't get swept up in the adrenaline rush and lose sight that you are considering one of the biggest purchases of your life.

Agents Are Out to Get You

There are a lot of good people in the trades. But it has been my experience (and is widely agreed) that people who make their living in real estate – agents, brokers, mortgage brokers, etc. – are out to get you.

Of all of these, real estate agents are my least favorite.

I'm reminded of the Charlie Munger quote, "Show me the incentive and I'll show you the outcome."

The money circulating around real estate is enormous. Most of us don't otherwise handle transactions in the 100s of thousands of dollars. And when someone is compensated purely on a percentage basis of the cost of the home, their incentives are – at best – only loosely aligned with yours.

It's hard, but not impossible, to buy houses in the United States without an agent. And how to choose an agent – or avoid getting one — is too long a topic for this article. But understand that "your agent" is not on your team.

Read How to Buy A Used Car

Read "How to Buy A Used Car." There are a lot of similarities between buying a used car and buying a house.

Read *Abundance* – and Know That's Not The World We Live In

Ezra Klein's book *Abundance* is a hopeful picture of what the world might look like if we were to build in the United States. And it isn't the world we live in.

Instead we live in a world where the accelerated rate of change exists in stark contrast to the slow tedium of hundreds of years of bureaucratic process.

Even as technology enables us to move and think faster than ever before in human history, the lethargy of governmental bureaucracy stagnates growth.

Unfortunately, that's how it is right now. Plan accordingly.

Conclusion

I'm thrilled with our new home, and the sensation of being a first-time home buyer. But perhaps even more importantly, I'm no longer overwhelmed by an industry that previously felt impenetrable, overwhelming, and ridiculously complex.

Hopefully this article is a first step for you to achieve the same.

HOW TO GO DOWN A RABBIT HOLE

*Originally published
March 2025*

Three weeks ago, my girlfriend and I were looking at rentals just south of San Francisco. Over the course of a long afternoon, we looked at seven different properties.

The next evening, she messaged me a new Zillow listing – this time for a property for sale.

I walked over and wrote her a note: "Fuck it, let's buy!"

What followed were weeks of going deep down a new rabbit hole. I spoke to hundreds of people, interviewed friends and family about real estate, and we put in four offers on a house.

The World Is Too Loud

In a world rife with distraction, falling down a new rabbit hole isn't always escapism. Sometimes it's how we survive.

The allure of breaking news, the infinite scroll of a social feed... Amidst the chaos of modern life, the ability to go deep – to immerse yourself completely in something new – isn't just useful. It can be a source of sanity.

The Sanity Of Obsession

When the world is chaotic, most of us turn to distraction – even when those distractions leave us feeling worse.

Early in the COVID-19 pandemic, I watched some of the Netflix Documentary Tiger King. While it was a welcome distraction, I came away feeling buzzed and empty.

By contrast, a true rabbit hole – one with structure, challenge, and stakes – isn't escapism.

My world view changed when I walked into a gymnastics gym at 17 years old and began to learn gymnastics. That rabbit hole has consumed me ever since. Similarly, when I studied ballet obsessively for a year, founded Responsive Conference to study the future of work, or started Zander Media to practice storytelling.

Deep learning is a way to regain control over your attention and expand your world view.

Learning is often conflated with speed, with getting more done in less time. I have studied speed reading, memory palace memorization, and other learning "hacks," but what interests me more is depth, breadth, and languor.

But my goal with real estate wasn't just speed. It was depth. Amidst the chaos of the world, it was restorative to spend a few hundred hours researching with ChatGPT, calling dozens of realtors and brokers, interviewing friends, and immersing myself in a new discipline.

Finding Your Rabbit Hole

Here are two questions I've been finding it useful to consider when embarking on a new learning journey.

Why This?

My girlfriend and I were ready to buy our first home. There was a specific house that we were interested in. And, as a friend said to us, "You have to live somewhere."

That question will guide your rabbit hole learning journey.

Why Now?

With real estate, we had a very clear rationale.

There were several options available to us — including renting for a year, a short term rental, or finding a house very near term that we wanted to buy.

What's Your Deadline?

I'm a proponent of external deadlines. Without deadlines, I will put off until next month something that I could equally accomplish this afternoon.

But when I have a deadline — a person I'm accountable to, a place that I want to live — I'm capable of more than I'd previously have thought possible.

Why Rabbit Holes Matter

The world is chaotic. There's more distraction and noise on the front page of any news outlet or social media platform than any of us should be consuming.

Deep learning forces us to focus on depth — on something that actually matters. And in a world that's only getting noisier, that kind of focus is how we stay sane.

HOW TO CLIMB A MOUNTAIN

Originally published April 2025

I spent a lot of my childhood scrambling up and down mountains. When I discovered this metaphor at 13 years old it resonated for me – and still does today. The idea is that you need to get to the top of a mountain, and there are two different ways to do so.

Two Different Approaches

You can plot, and plan, and spend months studying a challenge. You can walk the circumference of your mountain. Study it from every angle, consider potential routes, and plan your ascent. And then you take a single trip up the mountain – and hopefully succeed.

Or you can do the opposite, and study your mountain while attempting to climb it.

You'll almost certainly fail. You might even fall down. But every day, you get back up and throw your full capacity against the challenge until you might eventually succeed.

Both of these approaches are valid. There isn't one correct approach to tackling a challenge.

My Real Estate "Mountain"

I've just completed eight weeks of intensive study of real estate. I've never learned so much in such a short period of time in my life before!

Last week, my girlfriend and I backed out of escrow. While I'm still waiting to get my deposit back, we've emerged largely unscathed.

This article isn't an argument for throwing yourself at a problem, and learning on the way. It is an articulation of these two choices, and why I tend to operate the way I do.

The Dangers Of Overthinking

I'm very susceptible to analysis paralysis. I'll come up with two opposing perspectives and get stuck between them. To avoid this indecision, I've learned to take action by default. I throw myself at a problem and trust my ability to learn on the fly.

In real estate, this meant finding a property we were interested in, learning enough to put an offer on the house, and then sprinting to learn everything I needed to know to make an informed decision.

The Downsides Of Haste

When you're climbing a mountain that's too difficult for you, you're more likely to get injured.

When I throw myself at a problem, I'm more likely to make mistakes or offend people than if I'd spent months or years studying the subject. I can be less prepared than I might like, even when preparation is a winning advantage!

At the end of our real estate sprint, my girlfriend and I are both exhausted. The only arguments we've ever had have been about real estate.

The Benefits Of Speed

But the advantage of quick, decisive action is also significant.

We attempted something that neither of us would have otherwise considered. We didn't get stuck in indecision; we took decisive action.

And, fortunately, backed out before we found ourselves in a difficult situation.

Finding Your Way Up The Mountain

The two different ways to navigate a challenge are a choice between preparation and speed. There isn't one correct balance of preparation versus speed—only the balance that best suits you.

I'm more likely to charge headlong into a challenge. Here's how to assess what's best for yourself:

What's Your Default?

Reflect on whether you gravitate toward preparation or more immediate action. If you usually plan carefully, try taking small risks. If you tend toward immediate action, try pausing occasionally to strategize.

Reflect And Iterate

After completing a big project, reflect on what worked and what didn't. Which approach did you use, and how effective was it?

Through every challenge, we have a choice for how to tackle something difficult. Ultimately, it's nobody's responsibility but your own to decide how you'd like to tackle your next big mountain.

HOW TO TILT AT WINDMILLS

Originally published
April 2025

In *Don Quixote* by Miguel de Cervantes, Don Quixote believed the windmills were monstrous enemies threatening the land. He charged the windmills and was, of course, knocked off his horse by a windmill's sail.

This is where the phrase "tilting at windmills" comes from. It means fighting futile battles.

My Real Estate Battle

I've spent more than 600 hours over the last two months learning about real estate. My girlfriend and I want to buy a home, and I've rarely had more ridiculous fun.

Just this week I discovered documents from 2019 that show the extensive work still required by the County of Marin. Among 50 other items, these plans call for structural re-engineerings and sprinklers to be installed throughout the house.

I discovered this report, which appears to be the nail in the coffin in our bid to buy the property, less than 24 hours before it was too late. Reading it, I said goodbye to this project and property.

But the next morning, for the joy of the game, we submitted a new offer detailing our findings and requesting a 25% reduction in price.

Instead of laughing, the seller asked for more details.

Real Estate Is Broken

More than nonprofits, education, or even politics, real estate is a broken system. It is where good ideas and dreams go to die.

Had I not put in more than 600 hours in the last eight weeks, I would find myself the proud owner of a new home only to discover – to my horror – that a million dollars and several years are needed before we can take occupancy!

Fortunately, discoveries made in escrow have to be disclosed to future buyers. Even after I walk away, I've done a service to whoever does eventually buy this property.

I'm not going to be able to change a system that makes navigating bureaucracy twice as costly as doing actual renovations. I am not even attempting to change that system. But I am trying to make my small mark.

Navigating Broken Systems

We're living amidst broken systems.

In the United States, in the last hundred days we've witnessed a collapse of "norms" that I was taught were laws of the land.

The US government can deport people who are in the United States legally to El Salvadoran gulags, and the courts, lacking physical threat of force, are powerless to stop it. I feel pretty helpless to do much about the state of the world.

Relentless Optimism

A friend this week asked me what I do to keep positive amidst as much challenging news as there is in the world today.

I answered that I cultivate relentless optimism. I choose my battles carefully. And then, occasionally, I go to war with windmills.

How To Tilt At Windmills

Identify Worthy Windmills

Not every battle is worth fighting. But some – even unlikely ones – align with your values, stretch your capabilities, and help you grow.

Enjoy The Process

Even if the immediate outcome isn't guaranteed, attempting the practically impossible builds resilience. The journey is the reward.

Practice Optimism

Optimism is a practice. Make it a habit to celebrate small wins and find opportunities in setbacks. Optimism isn't naïveté. It is strength in the face of adversity.

I don't think we'll buy this property. I'm nearly to the point that I want to walk away. But perhaps we all ought to spend a bit more time tilting at windmills.

3

SALES & STORIES

HOW TO SELL

*Originally published
August 2023*

Everything in life is sales. From inviting your child to do her homework, to deciding where to go for dinner, to encouraging a colleague at work, the situations we encounter daily are filled with the dynamic of sales and persuasion. And, unfortunately, most of what you know about sales is wrong.

What Is Sales?

My favorite example of sales comes from a scene from the classic Christmas movie Miracle on 34th Street.

In Miracle, the Macy's department store Santa asks each child who sits on his lap what they want for Christmas. Santa then tells the family where they can purchase that toy at the best price, even if it means at a competing department store. At first, the store manager is outraged that Santa is supporting his competitors – until he sees enthusiastic customers returning to Macy's because of the excellent customer service. The value to Macy's of Santa's recommendations is greater than the sale of a single children's toy; its customer loyalty.

Sales is having a clear solution – a service, opportunity or opinion – that can help to solve somebody's problem. Like Santa, good sales means aligning yourself with the interests of the person you are talking to, to discover if your solution is a good fit for them. If it is, invite them toward your solution, and if not, move on.

How To Do It Wrong

Sales and persuasion are most often practiced with pressure and urgency.

Think of the reputation of a car salesman – pushy, fast-talking, deceptive. They aren't considering what is best for the customer. They only want to sell a specific car at the best possible price. The result: nobody enjoys the experience and the customer won't recommend that product or service in the future.

Pressure and urgency can work, but only in the short-term. They don't increase trust or loyalty.

How To Do It Right

A Process of Discovery

Done well, sales and persuasion should be a process of discovery. Instead of using force, inquire about what your friend wants to eat for dinner. Get curious about why your colleague doesn't want to do the work assigned to them.

When you start by asking questions about what someone is looking to solve – for themselves, their business, or their family – you'll discover if what you are selling is a good fit for the other person.

People relate through the stories that you tell them, so share your experience, too. As I discussed in the article "Everything is Storytelling," your story should be brief, personal and relatable.

Useful Beliefs About Sales and Persuasion

Abundance – If the person you are talking to doesn't want the solution you are offering, somebody else will. There are between 7 and 8 billion people in the world today. If the person you are talking to is not a good fit, move on.

Believe It – Believe in what you are selling. That doesn't mean that it is valuable to every single prospective buyer, only they can tell you that. But believing that it is valuable in the world makes closing easier, genuine, and fun.

Decrease The Stakes – There are very few game changing moments in life, and this specific sale isn't likely to be one of them. Whether or not you make this sale today isn't likely to matter over the course of your or your customer's life.

Autonomy – Foster the belief that everybody knows what's best for themselves. You aren't trying to convince anyone, but rather inviting them to entertain if what you're offering is a good fit for them.

Look For "What I've Learned" – It is useful to hold that even if you don't close a sale, you will have learned a lot along the way. This practice of iteration and repeated repetitions will make you better at closing future sales.

Put In The Reps

Improving at sales is a matter of practice and incremental improvement. Many of the most successful salespeople and deal makers in the world have practiced tens of thousands of times. Sales is as much a performance as trying out for a sport or auditioning for a play, and practice makes for consistency.

Your Attitude Closes Deals

Who you are and how you show up with a prospective customer is what will determine whether they buy. Who you are closes deals.

Maintain an attitude of enthusiasm and want what is best for the other person. You'll have a better chance of having things go your way.

Next time you are debating with your spouse about the dishes, trying to get your child to do their homework, or asking an employee to fill out their hours, think of Santa, sitting in Macy's department store, referring customers to the competition.

HOW TO TELL A GREAT STORY

Originally published February 2024

I've told the story of starting Robin's Cafe with no experience and selling it on Craigslist hundreds of times.

What's funny is I'm actually most proud of the culture we built behind the counter, the amount of learning I went through in learning to operate the cafe, and the role the cafe played in creating community in that neighborhood.

But when I mention selling a restaurant on Craigslist, I invariably get a laugh. "Craigslist?" People ask, incredulous.

Stories are the reason people buy from us – our ideas, our services, even our avocado toast. In order to sell, you need to tell a great story.

Everything Is Storytelling

You are already telling stories all the time.

- Hiring requires telling a story about your company.
- Deciding what movie to watch with friends requires telling a story about your point of view.
- Persuading your kid to eat their broccoli means telling a story about that oh-so-delicious vegetable.

The stories we tell ourselves become how we think of ourselves and the stories we tell others define those relationships.

The first step to telling a good story is to recognize that you already are.

Try This

Take note of a story you've told recently. I like to do this during my morning journaling. Take two minutes to note down a story that you told someone yesterday.

See What Sticks

The parts of a story that matter most aren't necessarily the things that matter to your audience.

When it comes to Robin's Cafe, I'm more proud of having opened up a restaurant in 3 weeks, but that tends to fall flat. I'm proud of the culture we had behind the counter, but without experiencing it, that's not of great interest to the listener. The moment I get a chuckle is when I share that I sold the cafe on Craigslist.

You aren't telling a story for yourself, but for the person you are talking to.

Try This

Look for reactions. Aspects of your story will land and other parts won't. That's useful information! Save the parts that elicit a reaction for your next telling.

Notice What Stories You Already Tell

In 2020, I moved into a house in the woods with my partner. Within a couple of weeks, my partner was parroting back to me a handful of stories that – apparently – I told all the time on Zoom. I hadn't realized that I was repeating so many of the same stories on different calls!

Even if you aren't aware of it yet, you are telling other people stories all the time. Pay attention to those stories, and use them as fodder as you refine your narrative.

Try This

When you are beginning to sell something new — as sophisticated as a new business or as simple as asking a friend to lunch — write down a list of possible stories that might help you accomplish your goal.

Refine And Hone Your Stories

We take for granted that a comic has to practice their jokes, or an athlete their sport, thousands of times for every single performance. It is less obvious that storytelling, too, is a craft.

Every time you tell a story is a chance to iterate and improve your storytelling craft.

Try This

Try telling a story in a subtly different way. Add a new variation or detail, and notice how your audience reacts.

Emotion > Rationality

When we foster connection with another person, we create the opportunity for change.

Facts and figures are great, but they don't accomplish much without the wrapper of a good story. To get someone even just to listen to your data, you have to form an emotional connection.

We like to tell ourselves that we are rational, but most of our behaviors come down to emotion.

Try This

As you head into your next meeting or difficult conversation with your spouse, ask yourself how you want them to feel.

We don't get to control another person's emotions, but just considering how you'd like for them to feel will influence how you show up and the course of the interaction.

A good story doesn't guarantee a successful sale, but without a good story your attempt to sell probably won't work. Storytelling is necessary, but not sufficient.

Hone your storytelling skills, by noticing and improving the stories that you already tell, and you'll be better able to move your audience – and your objectives – forward.

HOW TO GET STARTED IN SALES

Originally published February 2024

In 2016, I was given an amazing opportunity to take ownership of a global community called Responsive.org. After running my first ever business event early in the year, I decided to create my first business conference, Responsive Conference, 9 months later.

I'm a circus performer. I had never attended a business conference – not to mention produced one – so that first year of selling tickets to Responsive Conference was a madhouse.

That was also the same year that I started Robin's Cafe, so any moments that were not spent behind the counter, or hiring and firing baristas, I was on the phone with everybody I could think of asking for advice.

This distinction is key: I wasn't initially trying to sell tickets. Instead, I asked for advice.

Ask For Advice

I brought 275 people to Responsive Conference 2016 by asking people for advice. It is really that simple.

I turned to the founders of Responsive.org, everybody who had come to my free event earlier in the year, and everyone else I could think of.

When you ask for advice, you create the opportunity for excitement and support from people who might not otherwise be open to purchasing. People get enthusiastic about your cause, regardless of whether they're interested in spending money – or attend my conference.

By asking for advice, you create advocates who want to see you succeed.

Practice Your Story

One of the things that making those hundreds, even thousands, of calls in the first months of Responsive Conference gave me was practice telling my story.

I was new to Responsive.org. By luck and good timing, I was able to bring together 150 people for a free event at the start of the year and there was a lot of interest in our topics. But I was no expert!

By asking everyone I could think of for advice, I got a lot of practice telling the story of the ecosystem and why I wanted to create Responsive Conference.

Build A Network

When you are beginning to sell something new, you probably don't have a network or a reputation.

What you lack in network you can make up for in short calls with strangers. Ask everyone you talk to refer you to three other people. Quite quickly, the size of your network grows!

It takes time and effort to take calls with so many people, but you'll also go from no contacts to hundreds of potential prospects in a very short time.

The Final Step Is To Ask

The final phase of this saga, once you have enough experience telling your story and have built out a network, is to begin selling. Change your pitch from "Will you give me advice?" to "Would you be interested in purchasing a ticket?"

Several months into asking for advice, I'd talked with hundreds of people and generated a list of prospects in the thousands.

It takes courage to ask people to purchase. You can't hide behind the "I'm just learning how to do this" anymore.

The final step is to muster up the courage and ask, "Would you like to buy?"

Authenticity

This approach to learning how to sell something new only works if you are sincerely interested in what people have to say.

If you go into an "advice call" with the desire to sell, the other party will know and be turned off by the experience.

Be humble, stay curious, and look to learn.

Try This

If you don't need to, I don't recommend spending hundreds of hours on the phone with strangers asking for advice! That said, the practice of building a network is incredibly valuable.

This is the same process I use anytime I'm starting anything new.

Your homework is to call one person in the next two days and ask them for advice. The rules are simple:

- It can't be someone you normally turn to for advice.
- It can't be a topic that you've asked for advice for previously.
- The advice you're looking for can be business-related or personal, so long as it is real.
- At the end of the call, ask them if they would like to hear updates on your situation as it evolves.

And just like that, you've landed your first advocate.

HOW TO GET LEADS

Originally published August 2024

Your offer matters. The pitch you make about what you do and the value you provide has to be great in order for people to begin to be interested in your work. But in order to pitch you have to have people to talk to. You need leads.

Hand-To-Hand

Throughout my career, I've been pretty good at the hand-to-hand combat of selling through individual, one-on-one conversations.

This work is time consuming. It takes a lot of work! But it is also effective.

But, as a friend reminded me when I opened Robin's Cafe, nobody is ever going to care as much about your business as you are. If you want to build something, it'll help to get good at telling your story and making sales.

Word Of Mouth

I believe that most success in business – and in life – distills down to positive word of mouth. Your business grows when people talk about you to their friends. And when people bad mouth your work, your business suffers.

Even things like Yelp reviews or creating a testimonial video, where people speak to their positive experiences are just a distillation of this kind of word of mouth marketing.

There are a lot of ways to generate positive word of mouth referrals. But the simplest is just to ask people to refer you to their friends.

Ask For Help

One of my favorite ways to generate work is to ask for help. In the early days of Responsive Conference, long before I had any network or connections, that's how I started the conference.

That first year of Responsive Conference, with everything on the line and no experience to speak of, I asked everyone I knew who else I should talk to. Eventually, I started asking people if they'd like to attend Responsive Conference, too.

Asking for help backfires if you start selling too quickly or with any amount of pressure. Since you are asking people for their support, you have to remain humble and request support and assistance, rather than expect it.

Teach Your Customers To Sell For You

One concrete way of asking for help is asking your customers to sell for you. But most people don't know how to sell or to make referrals, so you have to teach them how.

These are the basic steps:

Tell Me Your Story

Teach your customers to tell their own story. A first person story is always going to be the most compelling reason for a prospective buyer to buy.

Where Were You Before The Product or Service?

Ask your customers to articulate to you where they were prior to use of this product or service.

What was their life like? What was the pain they experienced before they themselves purchased or tried the product?

What Changed For Them?

How did the use of your product or service result in a change for this person? And where are they now?

Finally, where are they now? How has their life or the problem that they had changed as a result of their experience with your product or service?

All your customer needs to do is share that personal story with others – to share the hero's journey of their transformation – in order to persuade new buyers.

Ask your customer to share their story of change with five other people

Do Free Work

I believe in giving work away for free – with a couple of caveats.

I broke this approach down in a video about how I took Zander Media from doing $1000 projects to $100,000 projects.

This is exactly how I started Zander Media: doing free work for people in return for their referrals. It doesn't always work

– I'd estimate that it doesn't work five times out of seven. But when it does, the payoff can be big.

While my accounting firm doesn't do free work in exchange for referrals, we're always looking for ways we can help partnering organizations by referring work their way, and generating goodwill.

Organic Content And Advertising

Nike has been receiving a lot of bad publicity lately because they've lost an incredible amount of market share and stock value.

As Trung Phan wrote about recently, this came largely due to a shift in Nike's leadership from a brand strategy to a focus on direct response advertising against their ecommerce platform.

Content that tells a compelling story, that gets people talking about you and your work, is hard to create and even harder to measure directly. Did a referral come because they saw a video or read a review? Even if you're able to ask them, most people don't even remember how they first learned about you and your service!

By contrast, advertising giants like Meta and Google make it easy to pay and then directly measure successful conversions.

Organic storytelling is much harder to measure but ultimately more impactful than ads. The value of a brand – people think of when they think about you – is more useful than the specifics of a single sale.

Who Else Holds Your Audience?

The most successful way I've sold tickets to Responsive Conference is through leveraging other people's audiences.

We have more than 30 speakers coming on stage at Responsive Conference 2024. Each of those people has potential people they might like to attend the conference.

As much as I am taking time to have calls with people who are considering attending – today I took a call with someone at the Secret Service, who is attending with her team – I'm also spending time with our speakers and partners, and helping them to promote the event.

Identify who else knows the people you are trying to reach. Partner with them to reach that audience.

HOW TO MAKE COLD CALLS

*Originally published
March 2024*

Two friends of mine recently started a new business, which we're affectionately calling BookBook.

It is a digital platform that allows users to display their favorite books.

The platform would display the spines of books, just like I do on my physical bookshelves. And the collections would only feature collections of books, like my favorite cookbooks or a list of what author Tyler Cowen calls "quake books."

Sourcing book spines turns out to be quite difficult. So I set out to phone book publishers in the attempt to find book spine designs for this project!

I took on this task of cold calling publishers because I love books, my friends are starting a company and I wanted to help. Really, though, I undertook this project to practice making cold calls.

Here are a few things I learned that will make your next cold calls easier.

Outline Your Pitch

The first step was to decide on my sales pitch.

I sat down with my friends and asked each of them to sell me on their startup. I recorded the audio of their sales pitches and took copious notes.

Then, I pitched my own version and asked for feedback.

We went back and forth like this until I had a rough script and was prepared to answer a variety of questions.

Outlining your pitch shouldn't be complicated. Decide what you are going to ask for and write a rough script. Bullet points are fine! Consider getting some feedback.

Then move on to the next step.

Set A Deadline

Practice enough that you are ready to deliver your pitch, but don't let practice get in the way of actually getting started.

Don't use preparation as a form of resistance. And don't forget Parkinson's Law – work will expand to fill the time allotted for its completion.

I scheduled a day when I would start actually calling publishers. That deadline gave me a concrete window in which to practice.

Set a deadline and give yourself a limited amount of time to prepare.

Rehearse Your Pitch

My next step was to rehearse my pitch.

I booked time in my calendar, because, for me, if something isn't in my calendar it doesn't happen.

During those rehearsals, I reviewed my notes and recorded a voice memo of my new pitch. Then I listened back, took notes and tried it again.

Hard things often take less deliberate practice than we think. But you do have to show up and do the work!

Make Some Calls

The final, and most critical step, was to actually start calling publishers.

On the day I had set aside, I Googled book publisher phone numbers and called all six of the big book publishers.

It would have been more effective to locate phone numbers in advance, but fortunately book publishers are easily available online.

This is the most critical step, because without actually putting in this practice, outlining your pitch, deadlines, and rehearsal don't have much impact!

Outcome

In talking to representatives at all the big publishing houses, I learned that book spines are even harder to source than I'd thought!

So while I haven't yet gotten access to book spines, I'm grateful to have taken on this small sales project as practice.

As people who have something to sell, we all want to be more comfortable talking to strangers. Likely the reason you don't ask more often is that discomfort and your fear of rejection.

And the best way to overcome that discomfort is to practice.

Most of us are uncomfortable asking strangers for things. But through this project, I put in the practice and took an incremental step.

Try This

Cold calling is one of the scariest things most people do. But that's because the steps are too big.

Get comfortable doing the uncomfortable thing when the stakes are low.

Today, pick up your phone and call one person spontaneously. Most people don't use their phones for phone calls, so maybe that's enough of a stretch.

If you do talk to people by phone, phone someone you don't speak to regularly.

See if you can stretch beyond your comfort and phone when you'd ordinarily text, or to contact somebody you don't normally talk to.

All the practice and rehearsal doesn't matter if you never pick up the phone and call, so just get started.

HOW TO SELL ACCOUNTING

Originally published
August 2024

For the last year, Zander Media has been on retainer with a firm that provides bookkeeping, accounting, and CFO services.

While most of what Zander Media provides for this firm is narrative strategy and content creation, at various points I've also stepped into a more active sales role, as well.

Do Great Work

The first, and most critical step in any business – any endeavor, really – is making sure that the quality of the work is great.

Without great work, no amount of marketing (i.e talking about it) and sales (i.e. asking people to buy) will result in success.

Good marketing of a bad product just leads to a faster failure. The first measure of any business is the quality of the product.

Develop Good Will

I am convinced that everything comes down to referrals. Even work that we don't think of as referral based, like Yelp reviews at Robin's Cafe or an abstract idea like the value of Nike's brand, condenses down to people talking about your thing.

And if all success in business comes down to getting referrals, the question becomes what is necessary in order to get people talking.

My answer: good will.

Whether we call it reviews, "brand," or just your reputation in the market, when clients think well of your business and tell other people about you, you're more likely to succeed.

What's Your Ideal Customer Profile?

Every business needs an ideal customer profile – a specific set of clients that they serve to the exclusion of all else.

As I've written about previously, there was a period when Zander Media did not target one specific type of client. We tried to be everything to everybody and, as a consequence, burnt out a lot of employees and goodwill.

Something as generic as bookkeeping can be for everyone. Everyone needs help getting their books in order and support preparing for tax season. But choosing your ideal customers is rarely a question of whether the services you offer can work for a variety of clients. Instead, it comes down to communication.

Is how you are communicating applicable and approachable to the clients they are trying to serve?

When you don't focus on a single ideal customer, you become generic. You speak in genetic language and offer generic things. And when you're too broad, you're not able to reach – or to serve – anyone at all.

Who Are You?

Early on in our work with this accounting firm, we set out to distill their organizing idea. We wanted to identify the core story that is unique to the organization and gets relevant clients onboard with their mission.

It's one thing to offer accounting. It is another, entirely, to have an offer so clear that relevant companies see, and then jump, at the opportunity.

I realized that our client didn't just provide accounting and financial services. They helped their clients understand what those numbers mean, and then use that information to shape strategy.

They focused not just on the numbers, but on the people behind the numbers who make the company work.

Make A Clear, Singular Offer

I recently read Alex Hormozi's *$100 Million Dollar Offers*. And while the entire book is worth reading, I particularly like the subtitle: "How to make offers so good people feel stupid saying no."

That should be the point of your marketing and your narrative. Develop a pitch so good that obviously your potential client is going to say yes to you.

If the quality of your work is subpar, see "Do great work" above. Good marketing has to start from there. But assuming you are already doing great work, you have to communicate a compelling offer.

How are you communicating about your work in such a way that the benefits to the buyer are abundantly clear?

In the case of my accounting firm this could be a variety of things:

"Make Sense Of Your Money"

Many small business owners have a lot of stress about their finances. Perhaps, they don't know how to read a Chart of Accounts or other financial statements.

This message is perfect when directed at a small business owner who is trying to make sense of their money.

"Take The Stress Out Of Accounting"

"Accounting is stressful!" This is a great message if your client is an early stage venture capital-backed technology startup that wants to focus on their core competency. They don't have to worry about bookkeeping and accounting because someone else will do it for them.

This message wouldn't work for a later stage technology company or larger privately-owned business. These companies know that an in-depth understanding of their finances can be a strategic advantage.

"More Money Than You Knew You Had"

This is a good message for a midsize business that is paying too much in taxes or not taking advantage of tax breaks. The owner or a Board of Directors knows they are missing out on financial opportunities to save or retain capital. This message is for them.

"Get Strategic With Your Finances"

This is for the CFO, Controllers, and more strategic side of the bookkeeping, accounting, and finances.

If a client is too small, or just plain scared about the state of their finances, this message won't resonate. However, if they know the value of a strategic view of finances, this is a message that can work.

Guilt Them Into Buying

If you have a lot of good will, a great reputation, and a clear offer that works for your clients, a potential client can't help but say "yes."

It is, eventually, important to ask people "Would you like to buy" what I'm selling.

But I'm a fan of providing so much value and goodwill up front that this final sale is a foregone conclusion.

You want clients who agree to buy from you because of the value – both real and perceived – that you've already provided them.

When you know exactly who you are selling to, and develop a great reputation, you can guilt clients into buying from you. Working with you becomes a foregone conclusion.

50% Communication

I heard a quote once that has always stuck with me: marketing is 50% doing great work, and 50% communicating about the work that you do. Making a clear, singular offer means communicating about the great work that you do!

Of course, then you have to deliver against that exceptional offer, too!

Next week, I'll take a deeper dive into leads and the various ways I've been helping my accounting firm get them.

HOW TO SELL VIDEO

*Originally published
April 2024*

I sat down with a Snafu reader recently who runs a one-man video production company.

In the five years I've been building my own agency, Zander Media, we've been in the fortunate position of handling inbound work, not cold calling prospects. I still have a lot to learn about selling video production.

Today's newsletter is for solo professionals interested in doing bigger budget work for high quality clients.

Got Milk?

I watched a MasterClass with Jeff Goodby and Rich Silverstein, the legendary founders of Goodby, Silverstein, and Partners. That's the advertising agency behind such icon marketing as "Got Milk?" and the Budweiser frogs.

Jeff and Rich discussed how they go about getting new work for their now 40-year-old ad agency. Jeff (or maybe it was Rich) describes pretending to be a journalist and talking his way into a fancy car convention in order to meet with a marketing executive at BMW to make a pitch.

Even having built and grown a 300+ person institution for decades, these two founders are not above entry-level tactics in order to meet the person they are trying to pitch.

Prior to this interview, I'd have believed that leaders as savvy and experienced as Jeff Goodby and Rich Silverstein wouldn't need to sneak into an event in order to sell to a new client. But it turns out that nobody is above selling, no matter how fancy their title or company.

This approach – going out and finding new clients – I'll call hunting. The other approach – cultivating existing clients; generating goodwill and referrals – which I'll call farming.

We'll tackle each in turn.

Hunting

In order to hunt, you have to first know who you are trying to reach.

It wouldn't have worked for Jeff and Rich to show up at a flea market and pitch their company. (Though I'm certain they'd have enjoyed that, too.)

They chose a very specific event, and one very specific attendee whom they were trying to reach. In short, they knew who they wanted to work with.

Most of us probably aren't going to target the Head of Marketing for BMW North America, but we can target specific people.

Choose a single, specific person you'd like to work with. Go hunting for them. You can always expand your audience later on.

Identify The Work You Want To Do

When my ideal customer sees an example of our work, they should be able to say "That looks like a Zander video!"

A video production company that does this especially well is Sandwich Video. Sandwich explainer videos are recognizable on sight – the bright colors, lighthearted demeanor, and the presence of their founder and CEO in each video.

What do you and your work stand for?

That mission statement might evolve over time, but you need a singular focus in order to be recognized and to stand out to your preferred customers.

Where To Find Your Customers

Once you know who you are trying to reach and the type of work you want to do, you need to find the customers who want that work done. There are an infinite number of ways of doing this, so here are just a few of my favorites...

Asking For Connections

Asking for help from connections has been the most impactful approach I've found to date for building any kind of business.

I wrote an article on "How to Sell with No Network or Connections" about selling tickets to my annual Responsive Conference. Also, watch the YouTube video about how I went from selling $1,000 scopes of work to $100,000 scopes of work in just a couple of years at Zander Media.

Asking for help goes a long way!

Events

Since 2014, I've run more than a hundred events on behavior change and the future of work.

If I'm not organizing an event myself, I try to set myself up to be an authority – by speaking, working at the event, or otherwise coming into contact with as many people as possible under favorable conditions.

Consider even just organizing a dinner or an un-conference targeted at the people you are trying to reach.

LinkedIn Sales Navigator

There are a wide variety of digital tools that provide you easy access to people, including LinkedIn Sales Navigator.

Most of the people you cold email won't want to hear from you, so you'll have to get over your reticence for contacting people who might not be interested. But LinkedIn Sales Navigator, and tools like it, allow you to reach out directly to the people you're trying to contact.

Cold Calling

The most extreme version of this approach is cold calling people directly, or even knocking on doors.

While you are likely to get a lot of "No, thank yous" in response, cold calling prospects is also the avenue that most sales people avoid or use poorly.

Most of us are scared of rejection and will go to great lengths to avoid asking people for what we want – and those who do use this approach rarely do so with finesse.

If you're going to cold call people or knock on doors, use it as practice honing and refining your pitch, instead of actively trying to close a deal with every call.

Farming

Farming is reminding your current and former clients that you exist, up-selling, and cultivating raving fans who will recommend you to their friends and colleagues.

Do Great Work

The first principle of farming is that you have to do great work. This is a good principle of business in general because without great work, the best marketing and sales in the world will just reveal that you have a terrible product all the quicker!

Promote Your Work

You should always be striving to improve the quality of your work — both in your delivery of the work and in how you communicate about it to your customer.

Doing great work that nobody knows about is doing a disservice to your potential future customers!

Ask For Referrals

Anytime, you deliver work for a customer, ask for referrals.

When a client walks away satisfied with the work you have delivered, it isn't enough to just anticipate or expect that they will recommend you in the future. As we know, most people are bad at selling, and referring work is a form of sales.

Towards the end of an engagement, schedule 30 minutes with your client and tell them that part of your business revolves around people — like them — referring clients to your business.

Keep In Touch

The best referral system in the world doesn't matter if you are not then top of mind for your customer. They need to be thinking about you at the appropriate time in order to hire you again or refer you to a likely connection.

My preferred mechanism for keeping in contact is an email newsletter, because everybody uses email. But this can also be through consistent social media content, videos, or text.

The key is to remain top of mind, so that your clients think of you at the right moment.

Surprise And Delight

Look for ways to surprise and delight your clients.

At the end of every year, I receive a handful of care packages from customers and clients, all with varying degrees of thoughtfulness and care. This is the same principle behind the ubiquitous startup branded hoodie and other swag.

But surprise and delight can be more nuanced. What's a little thing at the right time that can encourage or delight your customer?

A get well card for a sick child. A sports jersey to their favorite team. Thoughtful gestures that take time and consideration can have an impact for years.

Try This

It's easy to get overwhelmed by the number of things that can be done to improve your business.

The only recourse is to take one small step today every day towards one of the objectives, and focus on that goal every day until it has been improved.

Your homework is to pick a specific tactic from this list and write out the incremental steps towards its improvement.

What are a few small steps which will improve your client's experience?

HOW PIXAR TELLS STORIES

*Originally published
June 2025*

I had a call recently with Bobby Podesta, a 20-year veteran animator at Pixar. The call was supposed to be about Responsive Conference, my annual conference about work. Instead, we spent the entire time talking about storytelling.

I've been telling stories since I was quite young, but I've really only studied storytelling since starting Zander Media.

Bobby, a professional storyteller, crisply described story structure in four parts: the setup, catalyst, turning, and resolution. Bobby began his career illustrating comic books, so when he describes the four parts of a story, he references the four frames of a comic strip. First, each of these four parts:

- Setup – establishes the world in which we find ourselves
- Change – something new that disrupts the norm
- Turning – a twist or reveal
- Resolution – the payoff or conclusion

To illustrate these stages, Bobby told me the story of Steve Jobs' introduction of the iPod Nano – and the importance of a turning point in making Job's pitch both compelling and memorable.

Setup

Jobs walks through Apple's music strategy and the success of the original iPod. "We've got the best music store, the best software, and the best player."

Change

He announces a new product: the iPod Nano. "Today we're introducing a second member to the iPod family." He describes its features, shows a comparison chart, builds anticipation. But no actual product is visible.

Turning

Then, Job pauses, smiles, and asks: "You ever wonder what this pocket is for?" (He points to the tiny coin pocket in his jeans.) "I've always wondered that." Then, he pulls the iPod Nano out of that pocket. It's a dramatic reveal.

Resolution

The room erupts in applause. The narrative lands: Apple has not only made a new device. They've redefined what a small music player can mean.

As Bobby pointed out to me, this could have happened without the turning point. But without that moment of suspense and emotional engagement, it wouldn't be memorable. By pausing and asking a simple, unexpected question, Jobs completely changed the audience's experience.

4

WORK

HOW TO OVERCOME RESISTANCE

Originally published June 2023

We all have habits and behaviors that we acknowledge are important to do – and which we will come up with any justification to avoid. Cold calling a sales prospect, a difficult conversation with a loved one, or your least favorite chore.

I feel most alive when I do two things every day: my movement practice and writing. But, just as I procrastinate before getting into my cold plunge, I can come up with an infinite number of reasons to avoid sitting down to write.

I haven't written regularly since 2017, when I published *Responsive: What It Takes To Create a Thriving Organization*.

And the process of finishing Responsive was so painful that afterwards I stopped writing altogether. (Much of that challenge actually came because during that same period I sold Robin's Cafe while going through a very difficult breakup. It was a difficult year.)

This spring, I've finally built back my daily writing habit and recognized that the real reason I haven't written regularly is "Resistance," which Steven Pressfield coined in *The War of Art* to describe why we don't do our most important work.

In today's newsletter I'll break down some habits and tactics for recognizing Resistance, and next week I'll share habits for overcoming Resistance.

Identify Resistance

The first step is to identify Resistance.

It's taken me six years to realize that writing every day was something I was avoiding. Having identified that, I can now begin building habits towards writing more regularly.

Whatever the thing is that you've been avoiding, ask yourself if the underlying reason you're avoiding that behavior is Resistance?

What's Your Most Important Work?

You know the most important work that you need to do. When you find yourself coming up with any excuse to avoid taking that action, that's a good indicator that you are succumbing to Resistance.

Look for the moments of pride or excitement in your life. These might give an indication of what you could be doing more of.

One question to ask yourself is "What are the habits or behaviors that you would like to do more of – but aren't?"

What one action will move everything else forward?

In work, and in life, there are always a few actions that will have an outsized impact.

- the person you most need to call.
- an email that you'll feel relieved having sent.
- the sale you need to close.
- the unopened pile of bills to pay.
- the one food you need to cut from your diet.

Whatever the thing is that creates the biggest point of leverage in your personal or professional life, chances are, if you're not taking that action, the reason why is Resistance.

What are you already doing (at least in some way)?

Many of my proudest professional moments in the last decade have incorporated writing:

- publishing my first book, *How to do a Handstand*
- drafting the Craigslist ad that ultimately sold Robin's Cafe
- writing my first commercial script at Zander Media
- this book!

While I haven't published a book since 2017, or published on my blog consistently in years, I do write – and I feel good when I do.

How Does This Make You Feel - Afterwards?

Practice things that are hard, but that leave you feeling great afterwards.

While I love the taste of a good cocktail, I stopped drinking 18 months ago because I'd consistently sleep poorly.

By contrast, getting into my cold plunge is really hard beforehand, but when I get out, I feel absolutely fantastic.

Fear Is A Good North Star

Fear is often a good guide for what to focus on.

Of course, a fear of heights shouldn't automatically dictate that you take up BASE jumping, but there is always a kernel of directional focus behind what you are afraid of.

Follow Your Fear

What did you want to be as a kid? What did you want to be when you grew up? For me, it wasn't a writer, but a drummer or a professional skier. In other words, an entertainer.

The thing I like most about writing – or creating at Zander Media, for that matter – is creating content that helps people to connect and enables change.

While there isn't a one-to-one correlation between what you wanted to be and Resistance, there can be clues from your history.

HOW TO BE PERSISTENT

Originally published July 2024

When you follow up you demonstrate your character and your trustworthiness. And, anyway, we can all benefit from a few reminders.

The Value of Persistence

Few things contribute more to getting what you want than consistently showing up, courageously overcoming your fears, and asking for what you want.

When you get rejected, try again. And when you get told no, denied, or even scorned, use that rejection as a reminder that you are practicing persistence.

How To Be Persistent

Persistence can be learned. It is a habit, and like any other behavior, the best way to adopt it is through incremental steps.

First, decide that being persistent is something that you want to learn.

Then, look for ways that you can practice persistence in your daily life:

- Is there a skill you're trying to improve? Practice doing it one more time each day than you'd planned to.
- Are you trying to persuade someone of your world view? What's one small action in that direction?

The 2-Minute Rule

In his bestselling productivity book, *Getting Things Done*, David Allen teaches the 2-minute rule, which states that if a task can be completed in two minutes or less, you should do it now.

I prefer a 4-minute rule. If something takes less than four minutes, I try to do it immediately.

That doesn't always work. When I have a day of back-to-back meetings, I don't have time to do a variety of tasks in between. But as a framework, I follow my 4-minute rule whenever possible.

If you can, follow up immediately.

Practice Skills That Require Persistence

As I wrote about in the article "Specialization is for Insects", I love meta-learning, or skills that train other skills. That's why I like selling. Sales requires empathy, storytelling, and confronting your fears – all of which are valuable standalone skills.

I practice persistence by training towards a 60-second one-arm handstand. Handstands require a daily dedication to the craft, and very incremental progress.

Leadership Requires Persistence

I'm reading *Hero: The Life and Legend of Lawrence of Arabia*, and am fascinated by T. E. Lawrence's skill as a leader. I hadn't realized that T. E. Lawrence made a study of leadership.

So much so that when he arrived in Arabia, Lawrence had already cultivated the commanding charisma – not to mention the language fluency – necessary to lead the Arab revolt.

Leadership is the skill of doing little things every day to keep a variety of people taking action together.

Courage To Be Disliked

One of the reasons that we don't follow up is that we are afraid to be disliked.

Inaction doesn't feel like cowardice. Whatever's scary just feels like something that we'd prefer to avoid.

Fear is insidious. It can feel like a rational fear of rejection or self-recrimination. But fear is often the reason we don't take action. And the antidote to fear is courageous action.

If you take courageous action – persistently ask for what you want – someone is going to take offense. That's just the price for trying to be useful.

When You're Hesitant – Ask Why

There's a lot of pressure in the world today to "Just do it." From the Nike slogan to the popularity of men like Jocko Willink and David Goggins.

But when I try to pressure myself to do something, I feel awful. It just doesn't work. I can't accomplish something difficult without understanding why.

I'm often afraid to be persistent. When I'm selling something, I don't want people to dislike me.

When I'm asking someone on a date, I don't want to be turned down. But when I first spend a few minutes examining my underlying reasons, I'm often able to take action.

Persistence is a superpower. Following up is a skill that makes everything else you attempt much easier. And in the world today, we need more well-meaning people who persist and advocate for what they believe.

HOW TO RAISE MONEY

Originally published January 2024

In 2016, I started a cafe with no prior experience in less than a month.

Robin's Cafe is still in San Francisco today. And though I no longer get discounts, we should meet for coffee there sometime!

I had to raise $50,000 to purchase the assets I needed to start the business — espresso machine, ovens, tables and chairs. It was the first time I ever raised capital and I had to raise the money in less than three weeks.

Over that manic 20 days, I pitched more than a hundred people — and learned a lot. These are the tactics I wish I'd known then.

Know Your Business

I had lived blocks from Robin's Cafe for almost a decade. The neighborhood was long considered "the wrong side of the tracks," but in 2016 it was about to undergo a transformation.

When I opened the cafe there was a parking lot across the street. Today that parking lot is a children's playground. Startups were beginning to move into the neighborhood. 17th Street is now a thoroughfare for walking and biking traffic.

Starting the business amidst a growing neighborhood gave Robin's Cafe the momentum that it needed to succeed. Though I had never worked in the restaurant industry before, I had a competitive edge in knowing what the neighborhood was about to become.

Try This

Know your business. That doesn't mean that you are an expert on the entire industry (I certainly wasn't!) but you do need a competitive advantage.

What's yours? What is the thing that you see that other people don't? As you prepare to ask for money, focus on that.

Have A Clear Vision

My vision was simple: create a place where dancers, parents, local employees, and neighbors could eat and meet.

It helped that I was a member of many of the different communities that I wanted to serve: I was a community member and dancer of the building owner ODC. I was friends with employees of tech companies in the neighborhood. And I was a long time resident of the neighborhood.

In order to sell someone on your idea, you have to know the specifics of the vision.

As a member of these different groups, I was better able to communicate that vision and serve those groups.

Homework

What's your vision – the reason you are trying to raise money? Write it out as plainly as possible in two or three sentences.

Sell Your idea

As I started to ask for money, I talked to people about the decade I'd lived in the neighborhood and how I'd seen it change.

I walked people across the street to Mission Bowling Club, which is now a staple in the neighborhood, and shared the story of meeting the owners years before inside their gutted, abandoned warehouse.

I helped people see my vision for what this cafe could ultimately become – if only they'd be willing to loan me the money to buy the equipment I needed.

In order to raise money, you have to first get buy-in for your idea, which means you have to sell your idea.

Try This

Why should someone be interested in your idea? What's in it for them? Answer this question by listing out at least ten reasons why someone might be interested in the idea you are selling.

Share Your Emotions

I was determined to open Robin's Cafe within a very narrow window of three weeks because I was running a conference for 150 people in the same building and needed to feed my attendees. The entire idea for the restaurant came because I had the conference coming up and wanted to get coffee and lunch for my participants.

During those three weeks, I lived on caffeine and five hours of sleep – and I didn't try to hide my intensity from my prospective investors. Instead, I channeled that intensity into furor for what this business could grow into.

That excitement and optimism, combined with a sober assessment of the business opportunity, gave me the conviction to pitch the restaurant.

Try This

Share your emotions with your prospective funders – your excitement, optimism, and hope for what you are selling.

What are you excited and hopeful about? Tap into their eagerness to be a part of something bigger.

Show Them, And Don't Just Tell Them

At Robin's Cafe, I was able to walk people through the neighborhood and give them a taste of what the cafe could be – if only they would help with funding!

I shared my vision for what the cafe could be: a gathering space for dancers, for parents of kids, local employees and neighborhood residents. I walked my prospective funders through my landlord's building. (Fortunately, the landlord owns two very beautiful buildings!)

I made them samples of our menu and poured them free wine (conveniently ignoring the fact that I didn't yet have a liquor license).

Show your funders what the opportunity looks like. Help them to see the future that they are going to help you create.

Homework

Show your prospective funders the things they will experience. Give them the ability to put their hands on a product. Allow them to experience what you are selling.

Tailor Your Story To The Person

Fundraising is highly personal. Everyone, whether a professional investor or a personal friend, invests for their own reasons.

I showed off cafe spaces available for meetings and co-working to a friend who took meetings with clients throughout San Francisco, and mentioned that we could also cater their company's lunches.

There is an art gallery attached to Robin's Cafe, which I showcased to a local artist who was considering funding the business.

Try This

Learn why each prospective funder is most likely to invest before you pitch them. The more discovery you do, the more likely you are to succeed.

In the end, I successfully raised $50,000 from five people in under 20 days and successfully ran the cafe for three years before selling it.

I attribute that successful fundraise to three things: luck, determination and the decade of preparation I'd inadvertently put in while living and working in the neighborhood.

I don't know how to control luck, but incredibly hard work and a lot of research can make the impossible happen.

HOW TO CONDUCT AN INTERVIEW

Originally published September 2023

In 2013, I was invited to perform as an acrobat with one of the best operas in the world. Knowing nothing about opera, but with access to world-class performers I had 10 weeks to learn all I could.

In 2016, amidst the chaotic opening of Robin's Cafe, I interviewed more than 3 dozen restaurateurs and chefs with the hope of learning enough to keep my restaurant solvent.

Across my businesses and athletic pursuits, the ability to ask questions – to efficiently conduct an interview and learn from an expert – has been a very valuable skill.

Know Why

The first step to conducting an effective interview is to know what you are trying to accomplish.

As an acrobat in the opera, I wanted to make sure that I could perform my job within a storied and structured institution. My goal with restaurateurs was to learn as much about the industry as quickly as possible.

The first step is to begin an interview with a clear understanding of why you want to talk with this person and what you are looking to accomplish.

What's In It For Them?

Be clear about the benefit to your interview subject.

At the opera, even world famous operatic singers were willing to spend 5 minutes with a fellow performer when I approached them with humility and respect. Though I offered to compensate several restaurateurs and chefs for their time, they chose to donate their time for a brief interview. I paid them back by sharing the successes of the cafe and hosting a few of them at the restaurant years later.

Most people are happy to help. Some may want to see you succeed. Others feel good sharing their expertise. Communicate both your intentions and the benefit to them.

Setting The Context

Be deliberate in how to set the context for an interview. The more thoughtful and deliberate you are, the smoother the conversation is likely to go.

- Put your interview subject at ease – Don't jump straight into the conversation. Put your interview subject at ease by spending a few moments setting the context for the interview.
- Check in at the beginning – Check in at the start of your interview. Make sure that it is still a good time. By checking in, you demonstrate that you are able to lead the conversation.
- Start on time – Arrive early. Start your interview on time. Your promptness is a demonstration of your proficiency as an interviewer.
- Keep your commitments – Set expectations for the length of the conversation and then keep them. Better yet, end early.

Flow Of The Interview

This is your interview. Take responsibility for it! Here are some tactics to help you moderate the conversation and learn efficiently.

Do Your Research In Advance – The more time you spend preparing in advance, the better the conversation will go. You will be better able to ask intelligent and informed questions if you research your interview subject in advance.

Follow Their Story – You are there to learn from them. Don't interject or change the subject because you have an interesting insight or experience to share. Follow where your interview subject leads you.

Interject Thoughtfully – Be thoughtful with your interjections. Especially when time is tight, avoid interjecting your own stories. When you interject, you decrease the time your interview subject has to spend with you and you to learn from them.

Don't Let Them Get Into A Rut – Your interview subject may start to repeat themselves, monologue, or discuss things that aren't especially interesting or important to them – or to you. Redirect by asking a more specific question or something that is completely unexpected.

If You Are Bored, They Are, Too – If you are bored, chances are that your interview subject is, too. You aren't doing anyone any favors by continuing to ask questions when both you and your interview subject aren't engaged. Either move to another topic or politely conclude the interview.

A Word About Interrupting

Interrupting has a bad reputation because it is usually done with aggression or malintent. In situations where your interview subject's time is precious, interrupting them can be the fastest way to speed up the conversation.

My favorite method of interrupting is to say "I'm sorry to interrupt, but..." and then proceed to interrupt them. Preceding your interruption with a brief apology will often defuse any tension that might come.

Another technique is to set the expectation at the beginning of the conversation that you may need to interrupt the conversation in order to be respectful of their time.

Asking questions can speed up your ability to learn. To do this, you have to be able to efficiently interview people. Be thoughtful, efficient and direct in asking questions and you'll be surprised at how much you can learn.

HOW TO HIRE OFFSHORE

Originally published November 2023

When I was in third grade, my class was given an assignment: give someone instructions on how to make a peanut butter and jelly sandwich.

Of course, we all started with, "Take the jelly. Put it on the bread." And because we didn't tell them to take the jelly out of the jar first, we ended up with a jar of jelly sitting on a loaf of bread!

My early experiences hiring and managing people were a lot like that.

When I first read Tim Ferriss' *The 4-Hour Workweek* in 2011, I immediately went out and hired my first virtual assistant.

The several hundred dollars I spent to hire my first VA was, for me, a significant investment. I had no idea how to manage someone. Our communication broke down and within three weeks I concluded that hiring virtual assistants didn't work.

As it turns out, the high cost, my own inexperience managing, and the lack of time I gave myself to learn didn't make for a great first experience.

Unfortunately, this is how learning often happens:

- A bad math teacher leads you to the conclusion that you are bad at math.
- A bully on the basketball court leads you to swear off ball sports.
- Your first experience managing someone goes poorly and you conclude that it is your fault.

But more than a decade after learning that hiring virtual assistants doesn't work, I've changed my mind. Here are a few of the hiring habits I wish I'd realized sooner.

Learn To Manage People

The biggest mistake most of us make when trying something new is attempting the new skill once or twice, assessing (correctly) that it is not going according to plan, and concluding that this approach doesn't work. Worse yet, we often conclude that we are the problem!

I've found in hiring VAs recently that the key is to decrease the stakes and increase my time spent learning. Practice the skills you're trying to acquire before needing to get it right.

Habit: When you are hiring a virtual assistant, give yourself a set period of time to practice the skill of managing before making any conclusions about the success of the endeavor.

Lower The Stakes

The first mistake I made when I hired my first virtual assistant was to focus on the outcome. I wanted my VAs to do a great job and to save me time and money from the very beginning.

But that is not how learning works.

Instead, focus on what you have set out to learn, and don't expect perfection on the first try. When you expect that the work will have some challenges from the beginning, you will give yourself more opportunities to learn.

Try This

When you are undertaking a new project, like hiring virtual assistants, set aside part of your time and budget for learning. A "learning budget" if you will. Instead of assessing progress right away, give yourself at least a few weeks to acquire the skills of management and leadership you need for longer-term success.

Know What You Are Hiring For

Knowing what you are hiring for sounds obvious, but has been one of my most frequent mistakes. In recent months, I've hired three teammates in the Philippines. I wrote out detailed job descriptions for each role, but when I shared them with a friend, my friend pointed out that it was still very unclear what I was asking the person to do.

Habit: Write a job description as if you were teaching a 3rd grader how to make a peanut butter and jelly sandwich. Make the expectations foolproof by writing at a 3rd grade level.

Expect It Not To Work At First

When I am learning a new physical skill, I expect to fail often. If I don't fail at least 20% of the time, that means I'm not making the task difficult enough.

But, somehow, when I'm doing something new at work, I expect my execution to be flawless. When it isn't, I get discouraged.

Hiring virtual assistants, just like anything else, might not work the first time you try it. Learn and try again.

Habit: When you assign a task, remind yourself that it probably isn't going to work on the first try. That's part of the process.

Just Begin

While I'm mildly frustrated that it has taken me a decade to realize that I can hire virtual assistants, I'm also amused that all those years ago, within days of reading The 4-Hour Workweek, I made my first hire. I didn't even have a business at the time!

The only way to learn how to hire, or do anything else worth doing, is to try. And the only way to try is to just get started.

Habit: Take one step, today - and everyday - toward the outcome you want.

Some Other Things I Wish I'd Known Sooner

Here are some other things I wish I'd known sooner about hiring virtual assistants internationally:

- You can hire people full-time for $2-10/hour. Compared to the San Francisco Bay Area wages I'm used to paying, these wages, which are fair elsewhere in the world, are revelatory.
- There is a subculture of folks around the world who work US time zones. I don't insist on this with my VAs, but it can be arranged.

- Hiring can be very low stakes. Each hire matters, especially for a small company like mine. But when you are hiring for relatively low dollar figures, there's more opportunity to focus on your learning.

- Volume and multiple tries really matters. As with anything, learning comes with practice. Hiring VAs overseas is a great way to get repetitions and practice in.

- Expect to sift through dozens or even hundreds of applications. Most people have only ever been on the applicant side of the hiring process. Get a glimpse of the other side of things when you post a job application online and get hundreds of applications.

- It takes investing the time to save time. The cost and time savings will come. But it doesn't happen right away.

I'm delighted to have realized that I can hire international help to run my business and also do simple daily chores like schedule travel.

Moreover, I'm pleased to have another opportunity to recall that just because something doesn't work on the first try doesn't mean it won't.

It might just mean that I haven't broken down the steps small enough. The key may be going back to the building blocks of learning and to try again.

5

EVENTS

HOW TO RUN AN UNCONFERENCE

*Originally published
August 2025*

An unconference flips the traditional model of a conference on its head: instead of a pre-set agenda, the participants themselves decide what gets discussed. It is deceptively simple, but it's also one of the most powerful ways I know to spark connection and create unexpected breakthroughs.

What Is An Unconference

An unconference is any event where the agenda is set by those who attend. The rules of an unconference are simple:

1. Whoever shows up are the right people
2. Whatever happens is fine

3. Whenever it starts is the right time
4. It is over when it's over

In less flowery language this just means ditch expectation and don't try to control the experience.

Flow Of The Day

After attendees arrive, an empty conference agenda is posted on the wall with time slots and a variety of meeting spaces. Leaders share a theme or question they would like to discuss and post it in a time slot. If you post a topic, it is your responsibility to turn up to that session and introduce your topic or question. If you are not hosting a session, you are free to attend whichever of the sessions you are interested in.

Attendees are encouraged to adopt any of a number of roles:

- Leader – who is facilitating each breakout
- Scribe – is someone responsible for taking notes for each group
- Nomad – give attendees permission to move between break-outs

The Law Of Two Feet

Everyone at an unconference is encouraged to practice the law of two feet. The law of two feet says that if you become uninterested at any point, you are encouraged to leave and join another session. At an unconference you are also invited to take breaks at any time, with the idea that it is sometimes in the breaks that the 'A-ha' moments arrive.

Roles & Responsibilities

There are three main components necessary to a successful event: recruiting, production, and a strong facilitator.

A Word On Recruiting

In my experience, it is helpful to have an extended network to help with recruiting, not just a single person. All other logistics can be handled by a single person.

Production

Among the organizers, someone has to be in charge of logistics, including:

- Venue sourcing and ongoing communication
- Setting the date

- Attendee arrival emails
- Day-of logistics
- Recruiting

Facilitation

A strong facilitator can make or break any event, but especially one with as fluid an agenda as an unconference. On the day of the event, the facilitator plays a crucial role. It is essential to have one strong facilitator overseeing each unconference, to welcome attendees and provide context for the event.

How To Facilitate An Unconference

Here are some tips, most learned the hard way over hundreds of hours of practice in the last two years.

Stay Centered

Despite having spent a fair amount of time on stage, I found myself getting nervous and feeling rushed in the hours leading up to a day-long unconference. My single biggest piece of advice for a facilitator is to arrive with plenty of time to spare so you won't feel rushed. You are responsible for the framework within which the attendee experience takes place. As such, staying grounded and centered is the single most important thing you can provide, even though in the moment it may feel like it is more important to make sure the space is set up or the coffee is ready.

Don't Participate

This one might seem odd. It can seem like the entire point of organizing an event is to participate. In my experience, doing so decreases the ease with which I was able to coordinate new sessions, lead an end-of-day wrap-up, and refocus attendees when necessary.

In my view, the facilitator of the unconference is there in service to the attendees. I have found it gets in the way of the attendee experience to actively participate in sessions and workshops that occur throughout the day.

Practice

The facilitator should practice before the beginning of the unconference. Review these guidelines for a successful unconference and be able to describe unconference rules from memory. Practice your welcome speech.

Incorporate movement

I have always found it very useful to incorporate movement into events. When we have short periods of movement interspersed with other kinds of learning, we shortcut the passive sit-and-absorb tendencies we all learned through the education system, and which have carried over into most events.

Conclusion

Events are a lot of work, and something I've learned to produce of necessity. However, in this hyperactive digital age, I'm convinced of the value of what Tony Hsieh calls "spontaneous collisions" – the value of people spontaneously crossing paths. If you're considering putting on an event of your own, I encourage you to do so. When we create a container – an event or gathering – we create the opportunity for emergent possibilities to fill the open space.

HOW TO RUN AN UNUSUAL EVENT

Originally published September 2025

Last week's Responsive Conference was the best event I've produced. Attendees have been raving about the experience, my team bonded in new ways, and I walked away without the post-conference crash that too often accompanies producing a big event.

One of the things we did especially well this year was incorporate alternative event formats into the conference format. Specifically, there are three atypical formats that I think every event organizer should incorporate.

Fishbowl

A fishbowl is a panel with 1-3 additional seats on stage. Your audience is encouraged to sit in that seat and join the speakers in conversation.

Why This Works

Fishbowls challenge the audience to stay engaged. Every time there's a new participant in the hot seat, the audience – even if they weren't fully engaged before – has the opportunity to reengage with the conversation.

This format also adds variety for the speakers. Most panels fail because panelists talk to each other about pre-planned topics or things they know too well. Regularly adding new people to the conversation changes the dynamic with each new attendee.

Best Case Scenarios

A fishbowl can work with four seats on stage, where one seat is empty for participants. At its best, though, there are five or six seats available, of which two are available to participants or the facilitators.

This session can work in a fixed seating format, but works even better when the audience is literally sitting around the speakers, while the speakers are facing each other in the middle. A literal fishbowl shape added to the intimacy of the experience for everyone involved.

Considerations

You need a strong facilitator – The first consideration is that a strong facilitator has to set the context for this format and keep people moving in and out of the hot seat (or seats). This facilitator needs to describe how a fishbowl works, and encourage attendees to join in. The facilitator can occupy one of the seats on stage throughout or facilitate from the side.

The audience needs to be engaged – a fishbowl only works if attendees participate. This requires the facilitator to encourage attendees to jump in. Some gentle facilitation may be required to make this happen.

The people on stage need to be engaged – this isn't an issue for most speakers, but participant speakers should know that this won't be a typical panel. Most speakers don't want to phone in the experience – they want to enjoy the experience! But a fishbowl is not a panel, and some speakers may be hesitant.

Interview-in-the-Round

An interview-in-the-round is a session where each speaker interviews the next speaker. It works like this:

- Speaker 1 interviews Speaker 2
- Speaker 2 interviews Speaker 3
- Speaker 3 interviews Speaker 4
- Speaker 4 interviews Speaker 1

Why This Works

Attendees want to hear from the speakers. In this format, they get 15 minutes uninterrupted from each speaker (assuming a 60 minute session), with another 15 minutes where that speaker conducts an interview. Assuming good speakers, it is always a good experience for attendees.

Best Case Scenario

Speakers have an intimate experience on stage, which then translates into attendees' experience of the session. Through intimate one-on-one interviews, they are able to go places that they wouldn't in a larger group.

Considerations

Unpredictable outcome – The "outcome" from an interview-in-the-round is unpredictable. There isn't someone in charge of summarizing the experience for attendees, so event organizers might feel uncomfortable with the experience.

Speaker egos – The problem with this format comes down to speakers' egos. It isn't a common format compared to panels, and as a result speakers feel like they won't be able to get on stage as much as they expect to. This isn't factual – in an interview-in-the-round speakers generally get more stage time than in a typical 4-person panel. But from an appearance perspective, they often feel like they'll get less limelight.

I've never seen attendees dislike this format, but speakers may have to be persuaded.

Unconferences

I define an unconference as any event where the attendees set the agenda.

Why This Works

Unconferences work because there is always more collective intelligence in a group of attendees than in a single person on stage. An unconference makes use of that collective knowledge by allowing the attendees to determine the agenda.

Best Case Scenario

The best case scenario for an unconference is that it channels the focus of an entire group and everyone walks away reenergized and with several new ideas.

Considerations

The problem with an unconference by definition is that speakers and facilitators aren't the highlight. This makes selling tickets against name-brand speakers and brands nearly impossible. An unconference can be a great experience for attendees, but is much harder to monetize.

Gatherings and events are a competitive advantage in business, especially in an age of AI. Our loneliness epidemic and the enduring popularity of books like *The Art of Gathering* both demonstrate that humans want to gather in new, interesting, and immersive ways.

Any kind of gathering is better than not, but panels and happy hours need not be the only way we do so, and these three alternative formats provide some welcome variation.

HOW TO CURATE A CONFERENCE

Originally published
October 2025

Whenever I curate a conference, I think about how people are feeling when they arrive and how they are feeling when they walk away.

When it came to Responsive Conference 2025, most people – regardless of political ideology – were coming in with some degree of apprehension. Whether anxious about politics, AI, or the accelerating rate of change in the world, most people I talked to throughout 2025 were nervous. The next question was to decide how I wanted them to feel at the end.

My word was "excited." I wanted them to feel excited for their ability to contribute. Hopeful. Ready to roll up their sleeves. My work was to curate an experience that helped people move from apprehensive to excited through the course of the 2-day conference.

I wrote a few weeks ago about my concerns that people were having too good an experience, and the accompanying need to let go of the outcome. The outcome that I curated – almost without knowing it – revolved around purpose.

Simone Stolzoff debuted a new talk based on his forthcoming book How to Not Know. Many attendees came up to me afterwards and talked about how much his talk on uncertainty shaped their experience of the conference. I loved the stories he told about choreographer Twyla Tharp, whose book *The Creative Habit* is a must-read.

On Day 1, I facilitated A Funder's Fishbowl with three venture capitalists about investing in startups amidst uncertainty. Perhaps the highest praise I received about that session was each of the VCs approaching me afterwards to share that they intend to use the fishbowl format in the future.

My former boss Vivienne Ming opened on Day 2 with a talk about "How to Robot-Proof Your Kids" – about how technology can make us better humans (and not replace us). As always happens, Vivienne's talk ended with a long line of people who wanted to ask her questions and share ideas. Vivienne's got "rizz."

I got on stage alongside Suzy Welch, author of *Becoming You*, and entrepreneur Shelby Wolpa, for a session on values and purpose in an age of AI. Suzy said that most people don't even know what their values are. As a professor of management practice at NYU Stern School of Business who has studied values for decades, Suzy pointed out that values determine much of our lives, but aren't taught, or well understood.

To close the conference, Eldra Jackson III brought the audience to tears with a talk about the importance of maintaining our humanity amidst constant change. Eldra was incarcerated for two decades and has dedicated his life to helping people inside the penitentiary system get and stay out. He brought gravitas and provided a perfect end to the show.

As we've collected feedback from attendees over the month since, conducted our internal After-Action Review, and considered what we want to do differently at Responsive Conference 2026, I've had no regrets. That was new to me.

Ten years ago, producing Responsive Conference was about logistics, ambition, and survival. This year's conference was fundamentally different. I was calmer and well-resourced. The shift I experienced mirrors my attendees' experience: moving from apprehension to excitement.

I wasn't just running a conference. This year, I knew why it existed. That clarity wasn't only professional – it came from the alignment in my personal life (I'm newly engaged. I bought a house. I'm happier than I've ever been.) And when purpose aligns across personal and professional work, execution is much easier. I've gone through the same transformation – from apprehension to clarity of purpose.

Attendees arrived at Responsive Conference anxious about politics, AI, and the pace of change. Through talks, workshops, un-conferences, and plenty of time to reflect (and play with animals), they rediscovered what they care about and what they can control. The conference itself was a live demonstration of moving from uncertainty to purpose.

The experience of Responsive Conference – or any great event – isn't just about content. It's about remembering why we do what we do, and how to do it better. Without purpose, everything is difficult. With purpose, everything gets easier. The antidote to chaos is purpose.

6

Chaos

HOW TO FAIL BETTER

Originally published August 2023

There are a lot of things about being an entrepreneur that I avoid, but one of the silliest is opening physical mail. When I was starting Robin's Cafe, I got a lot of mail - plans from the San Francisco planning department, legal documents, food permitting, alcohol permitting, pest control notifications, more.

I was so busy figuring out the day-to-day of running the business that I developed the bad habit of just ignoring mail and leaving the pile to build up on my desk for weeks on end.

When I finally got around to dealing with the pile, there was always a notice that I'd ignored for too long - a vendor I was late to pay, an IRS document I'd missed, etc. As we all do when a task is too big, I came to dread opening my mail.

Failure As Discouragement

When you fail at a task, the experience is often one of discouragement, and that discouragement leads to a diminished desire to attempt that same task in the future. As I discussed recently, success is usually tied to positive feelings and the release of dopamine.

Negative feelings often have the opposite effect and result in a feedback loop of negativity and failure. For me, that meant avoiding the mail until I discovered late bills, which meant I'd continue to dread opening mail and let it pile up further.

Failure is often a sign that the task you are trying to undertake is too big. A trick, then, is to leverage the cue of the negative feelings of "I can't do this" into action and try again, but make the next attempt different. One way to do this is to break the task down into smaller parts.

Make The Next Step Smaller

When you are overwhelmed by a new behavior, the easiest way to tackle it is by making the next step smaller.

I don't need to open and respond to all of my mail on the day it arrives. A small step is to open every envelope, even if I don't take the mail out right away. This small step moves things forward and makes the next steps – removing the contents, reading them, responding – easier.

Take your large goal and just take one small step in the right direction.

Create Positive Associations

I have a letter opener that I really love – it is a beautiful folding knife with an olivewood handle. I've learned, in the years since Robin's Cafe, that I derive a particular delight in opening mail with this knife.

Look for ways that you can create positive associations around the edges of the habit you've been avoiding. Positive feelings equate to feelings of success.

Play More

Play and self-judgment are antithetical. When we are being playful or curious with a habit, it is impossible to regard an outcome as a "failure."

The best way I know how to play – especially when I'm not feeling playful – is to get profoundly curious about the task I'm trying to accomplish. Another is to make a game of the process. Personally, I get delighted when I see weeks worth of dealt-with mail pile up in my recycling bin!

Look For A Step By Step Breakdown

You can almost always find a step-by-step breakdown of the task you are trying to accomplish.

Google "how to do x" or interview someone better at that thing than you are. If you've hit a roadblock and aren't sure how to make a task more manageable, someone else has likely solved this problem before you. In writing this article, I asked a few friends about how they handled their daily deluge of mail and got some interesting ideas I'll try in the future!

At Zander Media, I receive 10x'd less physical mail than I did at the cafe. And while there are still remnants of my avoidant behavior, I'm excited to reframe failure as a cue for novel action.

These days, I look for areas of my life where I've historically failed and replace the cue of failure with the understanding that I haven't made that behavior small enough, yet.

Try This

Now, your turn: what's something you've failed at, recently? Reply back and I'll respond with one idea for how to turn that failure into a learning opportunity!

HOW TO TRAIN FOR CHAOS

Originally published May 2025

Michael Phelps' coach, Bob Bowman, understood that the greatest athletes don't just train for performance – they train for chaos. Once he recognized that Phelps had the potential to be an elite level swimmer, Bowman started building unpredictability into Phelps' training.

When traveling for competitions, Bowman would misplace Phelps' luggage or swimsuit. During practice, Bowman filled Phelps' goggles with water so he would have to swim without being able to see. Phelps was forced to learn to count his strokes per lap so that even if he couldn't see, he would know when to turn. This particular training challenge paid off in the 2008 Beijing Olympics, when Phelps' goggles actually did fill with water. He still won gold!

Try Red Teaming

Red Teaming is the practice of deliberately stress-testing your plans, assumptions, and expectations by asking yourself: "What if everything goes wrong?" Instead of hoping things go smoothly, know your contingency plans so when the unexpected happens, you know how to react.

Most of us wait until disaster has struck to figure out how we'll react. As a result, we panic, freeze, and make bad decisions. Red teaming is the opposite – it's mental preparation for failure, so when things go wrong, you already know how to respond.

Before an important event – whether it's a presentation, a workout, or even a difficult conversation – spend time imagining everything that could go wrong.

HOW TO SURVIVE AI

*Originally published
March 2025*

Last week, I hit an inflection point — a shift in perspective that altered how I see AI, and will shape everything I do going forward.

My History With Tech Waves

I came of age amidst the rise of the internet and social media.

In middle school I was in AIM chat rooms. (Don't tell my parents, but I snuck into the "mature" chat rooms when nobody was watching.)

Facebook arrived on my college campus during freshman year. I joined right away, but was hesitant to share my face online.

In 2007, when a college friend showed me his first iPhone, I was skeptical. It didn't have a keyboard and felt flimsy in my hand.

When I moved to San Francisco in 2008, the world was reeling from the real estate crash. An industry that I'd been told my entire life was stable, bedrock, had dropped precipitously.

When I was training gymnastics at Stanford University in 2012, several of the guys I practiced with were in crypto and tried to encourage me to buy. I've since seen three crypto boom and bust cycles.

Pattern Recognition

I started Responsive Conference out of my own desire to explore the future of work, and many of these trends.

I've met world experts on trends that became commonplace just a few years later – remote and distributed work, diversity & inclusion, blockchain, and more.

We talked about AI on stage back in 2019! But something is different now.

Casual Early Adoption

I've been using AI in my daily work for several years.

Ten years ago in video you had to manually transcribe an interview before editing. Now our transcriptions at Zander Media can be done in seconds.

I ask ChatGPT to review my articles for structure, grammar, and semantics. I nearly always search on ChatGPT instead of Google.

I've known AI is important, but not taken it more seriously than I did the rise of blockchain and crypto, social media, or even AOL chatrooms.

My philosophy has been that of a casual early adopter, "Oh, look! The world's changed again. And I still need to train my handstands."

This one is different

Last week, I hit an inflection point, which happened for two reasons.

My girlfriend is a data scientist and through her daily work she already knows that AI is a tectonic shift.

Then, I listened to this conversation with Tyler Cowen, which I highlighted in Snafu last week.

In the interview, Tyler talked about the significance of AI, the differences between the major LLMs, and how he uses each of them. I was struck by how much I didn't know.

I was chatting with my father over the weekend, and casually mentioned that AI was going to be the next electricity. He said, reservedly, that he might agree. I've since come to believe that AI represents the biggest disruption any of us have ever witnessed.

Bigger Than The Printing Press

I believe AI is going to be bigger than social media, the internet, electricity, or the printing press.

A basic premise of Responsive.org is that the rate of change is accelerating. But just like humans aren't very good at understanding compound interest or logarithmic growth, we aren't good at comprehending what it means when a growth curve goes nearly straight up.

I'm not an engineer. I don't understand machine learning, deep learning, or the math behind LLMs. And I've never been caught up in a hype cycle before. I wasn't all-in on social media, even though I was there at the beginning, or crypto, even though I knew people who were.

But as a lifelong lover of books, I've always said that I wished I was there for the advent of the printing press. This is that moment.

My Commitment

In a world that is on the verge of disaster – climate, socio-political unrest, and more – AI has the potential to be the collaborator we need to solve these issues. Equally, these tools have the potential to manipulate and destroy us.

My new commitment is to use these tools every day. In my current research of real estate, I've 10x my rate of learning by treating ChatGPT as a thought partner. While everything I write in Snafu will continue to be my own, I'm using these tools to hone my craft.

At Responsive Conference, people have been talking about AI on stage since 2019. But in 2025 I want to give attendees a direct taste of these tools as part of the conference experience.

We're at the beginning of a new era. One that has the potential to be both awe-inspiring and terrifying. We're not just building new tools – we're building something smarter than ourselves.

How do we want to participate? How do we reinvent ourselves even faster than the tools that are learning from us? That remains for all of us to decide.

HOW I'M SURVIVING THE NEXT 4 YEARS

Originally published April 2025

SNAFU is an acronym for Situation Normal: All Fucked Up. The phrase was born out of the chaos of World War II, but it is just as relevant today. Snafu has become my shorthand for a world that's always been broken – and now is undeniably so.

Things that once seemed stable – governments, economies, industries – are changing too quickly for us to keep pace. Technology is advancing faster than any of us can adapt, which reshapes our job, relationships, and culture before we can adapt.

Rules my grandfather espoused – work hard, get a good education, keep your head down and things will work out okay – aren't just outdated. They're wrong.

For the last decade, I've curated a conference about the "future of work". The premise is that the speed of change is accelerating. That while work in the 20th century was about the illusion of stability, in the 21st century we are watching that illusion disappear.

Political and social unrest are on the rise. Economies are volatile. Climate change and AI have added new layers to that unpredictability. We're living in an era where the old rules don't apply, new rules haven't been written yet, and chaos is the default setting.

Resilience Is Safety

When things start to break down, most people – and most companies – look for stability. We all want something or someone to tell us that things will be okay. Stable jobs, trusted institutions, and a plan we can rely on.

Unfortunately, those are an illusion.

The people and organizations who will thrive aren't the ones who cling to a false sense of stability. They adapt. Resilience isn't about toughness, but about flexibility. It's the ability to absorb shocks and keep moving forward.

Resilience is the only real safety net left because we can't rely on institutions, stable career paths, or a predictable future. We can thrive only by learning to pivot, adapt, and get back up when we fall down.

Learn How To Learn

For most of human history, learning specific skills was enough to survive or build a career. We became blacksmiths, factory workers, software engineers, and then did that work for the next few decades.

That's not how the world works anymore.

The shelf life of knowledge is short. Industries are being reshaped in weeks, not in decades. What you know today may be obsolete tomorrow.

The skill that matters most isn't what you know—it's how quickly you can acquire skills and apply that knowledge. How quickly you can change your mind. The skill we most need to survive and get ahead in the world today is meta-learning, or learning how to learn.

Success is about mastering the process of skill acquisition itself. If resilience is the goal, then meta-learning is the most effective way to achieve it.

How I'm Surviving the Next Four Years

I have no idea what's going to happen in the next four years. Nobody does. But things are going to slow down. Here's how I'm preparing for the next four years.

Physical Resilience: Our bodies are the first thing that break down under stress. When I was in a car crash a few years ago, my visible bruises healed in a week, but it took my body nine months to really recover. The way I train for physical resilience is doing little things, every day, that are physically difficult.

I Move Every Day, train to increase strength and endurance, and spend a couple minutes more in a 200 degree sauna than is easy. I'm not chasing peak fitness. I'm chasing a body that can handle stress.

Emotional Resilience: Life is unpredictable. Just in the last month, one friend had a mental breakdown and another died. Grief, uncertainty, and failure are inevitable. We can't control them. But we can train how we respond. I practice emotional resilience by cultivating tiny habits that increase mental fortitude.

One of the best tools I know for emotional resilience is, amusingly, the physical challenge of cold plunging. Through cold exposure, I'm better able to handle the stresses of other, less intense, circumstances. Just getting into the cold plunge (or turning the shower tap to cold) is a victory.

Do More Things That Scare You

Mental Resilience: The key to mental resilience is brain plasticity and avoiding fixed ways of thinking. Do this by limiting your intake of harmful content and by practicing new skills.

The world is full of outrage porn. The business model of the news and social media is to keep you coming back for more. You don't have to detach from the world in order to limit the amount of content — especially outrageous or toxic content — you imbibe.

Additionally, practice things that stretch you, mentally. I like to sing. I recently started practicing the piano. I'm attempting to learn Darija (Moroccan Arabic). In short, never stop learning.

The world is not going to slow down. The chaos isn't going away. If anything, things are only going to get more unpredictable!

The only real strategy left is to become the kind of person who can navigate uncertainty with intelligence, speed, and a sense of humor about the absurdity of it all.

Snafu is about that process—learning fast, adapting faster, and finding resilience in a world that refuses to make sense.

7

Emotions

HOW TO STOP FEELING OVERWHELMED

Originally published September 2023

I spoke with an entrepreneur recently who described founding her startup as the loneliest of jobs. Elon Musk, somewhat more dramatically, said that "starting a company is like staring into the abyss and eating glass." Running Robin's Cafe was the loneliest job I've held. It taught me a lot about my own emotional management, which has made running companies somewhat less difficult.

Regardless of whether you are building a business, trying to get better at managing a tough situation, or starting something new, I approach emotional management in two stages: avoid the spiral and incremental growth.

What Is The Emotional Spiral?

Throughout the first few months of running Robin's Cafe, I lived in a state of overwhelm. With everything that needed to be done, there were nights that I'd finish cleaning the cafe after midnight and then sit alone in the dark, too tired to go home.

That's the emotional state I call the spiral. A state of overwhelm, of being upset about being upset, where it is impossible to make forward progress or to plan ahead.

How To Get Out Of An Emotional Spiral

Recognize The Spiral

During the worst moments of Robin's Cafe, I often called my best friend and complained that I wanted to close the business. She would remind me that I could, in fact, walk away at any time.

The reminder that I wasn't stuck — that I had the ability to shutter the business — allowed me to step outside of my emotional spiral and move forward slightly less overwhelmed.

I've described bystander apathy, the cognitive bias in which we assume someone else is going to take action. Just as the solution to bystander apathy is to remember that it exists, the path out of an emotional spiral is to recognize it. Simply identifying a spiral can serve as a heuristic to take action.

Take Incremental Action

One block from Robin's Cafe is another cafe called Stable Cafe, which has been around for a decade and functions seamlessly. On my bad days at Robin's Cafe, I would compare my business to Stable – and berate everything about my own small operation.

It is tempting to focus on goals and aspirations that are far out of reach, but the consequence is feeling bad about where we are. We amplify that which is at the center of our attention. Being stressed about being stressed results in even more stress! Take some small positive action to build momentum.

Begin by taking one small step in the direction you want to go.

Take Any Small Step

Sometimes you don't know what the right next step is. I didn't know how to start a cafe! As I've written about in "How to Conduct an Effective Interview," I had to interview a lot of professionals and then take some action. When you are in a spiral, take some action.

Don't attempt to solve everything in a single moment. Put one foot in front of the other. Make each step as small as possible.

If you try to do something dramatic, you are more likely to fail and resume your spiral.

Adjust Course As You Go

Think of a sailboat leaving San Francisco for Hawai'i. You don't leave the coast, point the ship towards the Hawaiian islands, and then stop navigating. You'll get off course.

The best way to navigate is to adjust course as you go. The best time to adjust your trajectory is while in motion.

There were a lot of difficult days building Robin's Cafe – moments of panic, overwhelm, and loneliness. The businesses I've built since then have gotten progressively easier. There are still incredibly hard moments, of course, but I don't stay stuck.

I have more mental and emotional fortitude, better habits to avoid the spiral and to get out quickly. I hope this framework will help you do the same.

HOW TO FEEL BETTER

Originally published November 2023

I've always believed that in order to acknowledge what's going well in my life, I have to first solve any difficult emotional situations. Over the last few years, I've come to realize that it is often more effective to focus on the positive, instead of first trying to solve the negative.

Instead of waiting for things to go just right, it's more effective – and more fun – to focus on what is already going well. Here are some tools that can help...

Celebrate The Small Things

By celebrating the small things that are going well – no matter how small they are – we get more practice celebrating. Don't wait for things to go well in order to celebrate. Practice and you'll be surprised at how quickly you feel good about seemingly mundane things in your life.

Try This: First thing each morning, write down one small thing that went well from the day before.

Flip The Judgment

I have daily practice with my best friend: we phone each other and inquire "Is there a judgment that you would like to flip?"

We pick a negative judgment – that we're holding about ourselves or in the world around us – and look for the positive.

If I'm berating myself for a misunderstanding with my mother, I'll look for ways in which that misunderstanding could be beneficial.

If I'm judging myself for pushing through an injury, I'll examine how that pain could actually be helpful and result in recovery.

By taking something that you are judging as bad and looking for the positive in that same example, you are "flipping the judgement" and practicing gratitude.

Try This: Flipping judgements requires a lot of mental dexterity, so start small. Pick something small that you are judging as bad. Write a few sentences about how that situation could, hypothetically, be beneficial.

Worst Case Scenario

Tim Ferriss popularized the idea of "fear setting" through this TED talk. The purpose is to identify the worst case scenarios, which usually turns out to not be quite so bad.

My worst case scenario usually ends up with me shitting my pants in public and leaving the country in humiliation. But even in my hypothetical worst case scenarios, I usually survive and learn from the experience.

For extra credit, you can also explore the Best case scenario!

Try This: When you're considering something you are scared of, ask yourself "What's the worst thing that could happen?" Write down a few of your answers.

What Went Well

What went well is my favorite among the many exercises Martin Seligman, teaches in his book Flourish.

Historically, psychology research focused on "abnormal" psychology or problems to be solved. More than 30 years ago, Seligman began researching and teaching tools that help everyone improve.

One exercise that Seligman teaches is "What went well." Very simply, the practice is to list out three things every day that have gone well.

The practice forces you to focus on the specifics of what has gone well. By bringing attention to them, you recognize them, reinforce them and make them bigger.

Try This: Write down three things that went well for you in the last day.

Feel Shine

In Tiny Habits, BJ Fogg coined the word "Shine" to describe the internal positive emotion we give ourselves when we've done something well. When we reward ourselves with that internal feeling of celebration, we create a positive feedback loop. For more on Shine, here's an article on the topic from TED.

Try This: Take 2 minutes and deliberately feel good about something you've done today. Pat yourself on the back, pump your fist or smile in the mirror.

Look For Awe

I was sitting in the sauna a few weeks ago and struck up a conversation with UC Berkeley Professor Dacher Keltner, who has spent his career studying awe.

As we began to talk about his research I was reminded of the life changing moment when I first saw the circus. My parents took me to see Cirque du Soleil's Alegria, shortly after I began studying gymnastics at 17 years old. Watching the acrobats opened my eyes to what the human body is capable of and led to the last few decades of my movement career.

Awe has the capacity to fundamentally change our perspective and widen our world view.

(I'm also going to attend the professor's last class of the year next week. I'll report back)

Try This: Seek out awe. Whether through a beautiful view, over a meal with family or in listening to great music, look for an experience of awe. When you open yourself to the feeling of awe, you're more likely to experience it.

As you spend time with friends and family this holiday weekend, or go about your life, I hope one of these tools is helpful.

HOW TO USE FEAR AS A GUIDE

*Originally published
April 2025*

For many years now, I've repeated a phrase to myself: "Fear is my north star."

Fear is often misunderstood as a negative emotion – as something to be avoided. Instead, it is a useful guide for action.

Some of the most significant moments in my life came as a result of moving towards fear.

I'm currently at one of those crossroads in my life, so in today's Snafu article I'll spell out my approach to fear.

The Fear Of Opening Robin's Cafe

I will never forget a pivotal moment in April 2016 outside of what became Robin's Cafe.

I was on the phone with my friend Ronda, discussing all the reasons why opening my little restaurant might be a bad idea.

Ronda asked me a question that has guided me ever since: "Robin, is there any reason not to open up Robin's Cafe besides your fear?"

I paused for a moment, answered definitively "no," and from that moment was committed.

What Fear Has To Teach

Fear is one of those topics that we think we understand, but most of us never study. We see someone doing an act of bravery – a firefighter running into a burning building or Alex Honnold freeclimbing El Capitan – and call that courageous.

But what do those things have to do with our day-to-day, and what is fear even for?

Fear is a signal that something important is going on. That's it. It is a spotlight that focuses attention on a moment, a decision or a significant act.

When we attend to that fear, and examine it instead of running away from it, we give ourselves the opportunity to accomplish something more.

Fear As A Compass

There's another kind of fear worth mentioning: fear of true danger.

If I were to try to free climb El Capitan, I'd be terrified. I'm an experienced mountaineer, but have zero experience free climbing technical routes. About ten feet up, I'd be sweating.

Inexperience or fear of the unknown – even a child's fear of the "monsters under the bed" – might fall into this category.

But that's different from informed, and constructive fear – fear that comes from uncertainty and vulnerability, which can serve as a guide.

Whenever I feel fear about something that isn't imminently life-threatening – starting a business, making a big investment, or entering a new relationship – that's a sign that I'm on the right track.

The Fear Of Buying A House

I'm at another crux right now. Last week my girlfriend and I signed and put earnest money down on a house just north of San Francisco.

The house is a "fixer," being sold by a bank because the previous owner died. We'll need to do substantial work just to make it habitable.

We've run the numbers, paid thousands of dollars to have it inspected, and I'm in a moment of trying to decide if there are enough reasons not to buy the house, or if I'm just afraid.

How To Use Fear As Your North Star

Here are some useful tools in assessing fear that I've found myself using a lot in the last few weeks.

Name Your Fear

In real estate, I've been listing all of the potential outcomes that I'm afraid of. Seeing them written out on a page makes the fear more tangible.

Assess Your Fear

In business and now in real estate, I try to plan for the worst case scenarios.

What would happen if the housing market crashed? If we needed a new roof? If we couldn't cover our mortgage?

It's easy to be positive and hopeful about things going well. Planning for the absolute worst-case scenarios helps alleviate potential negative outcomes if the worst does happen.

Take Small, Incremental Steps Towards Your Fear

We've run countless competitive market analyses for this neighborhood. I've had five roofers out to inspect our roof and provide quotes. I've crawled through all of the attics to inspect the insulation.

Each of these was a single, small step towards a specific fear.

Courage Is Action Despite Fear

I define courage as action in the face of fear.

When I opened Robin's Cafe, I was afraid, but I had outlined all of the potential downsides I could think of. I don't know what will happen with our housing purchase. We may not get it, and we may decide to walk away.

But I do know that facing this fear – assessing it directly, breaking down the component pieces, and taking small steps – is a victory in itself.

Fear isn't something to avoid. It is a compass pointing you towards your growth edges and where you need to go.

HOW TO DEAL WITH PAIN

Originally published January 2025

I was violently sick with food poisoning on Jan. 1st. The challenge of that 12 hour experience has me thinking a lot about the benefits of relaxing into pain.

Throwing up is painful. Sitting in 34 degree water is painful. Even exercise, as much as I love a good runner's high, can be damned difficult.

But as I was retching my lungs up and cracking jokes to my long-suffering girlfriend at 4am, I was also reflecting on the best way to get through pain – and it isn't what you think.

As a kid, I jumped into a lot of snowbound lakes. I learned that the worst thing to do when swimming in freezing water is to tense up. Tension only makes freezing cold water hurt more, the suffering more unbearable. By contrast, when you relax and attempt to breathe through the pain, the difficult experience is… marginally less difficult.

The way through pain is to relax.

How To Take A Punch

I hope you never get punched. The best way to take a punch is to avoid it!

But the second best way is to tense up only just before impact. And only then as much as necessary to counteract the force of the punch.

It can be devastating to get hit when you're completely unprepared. But so, too, can tensing unnecessarily for an impact that may or may not ever come.

How To Survive A Car Accident

There's a weird phenomenon where really drunk drivers are more likely than the average to survive serious car accidents. They're so drunk that they relax in the face of a wreck, and are therefore more flexible.

(Hopefully it goes without saying: never drink and drive.)

During a serious car accident a few years ago, I recall relaxing just after the impact. As my car spun out of control, I let go emotionally, even while I slammed on the brakes. I credit that relaxation with walking away from the pile-up unscathed.

The detrimental consequence of tension

If you live in a constant state of tension, you're both less good at taking the hit, more likely to suffer when the impact occurs, and develop detrimental habits and physical patterning.

By contrast, when you learn to relax into discomfort, you remain more flexible. Counter-intuitively, you are more likely to get through the experience.

Sometimes, the best way through a difficult experience is by letting go.

How To Relax

Relaxing into physical discomfort is counterintuitive. You have to get enough practice to get comfortable, which means experiencing some pain along the way.

I've never seen someone get into freezing cold water for the first time and not tense up. You have to try it a few times.

But letting go in the face of pain is the same kind of relaxation as when you take your first sip of coffee in the morning or fall asleep at night; it is a moment when you let your stress drain away.

This is also the kind of determined letting go where I take a deep breath before I run the hardest hill on my 6 mile loop through the Oakland hills. I look up at the hill, turn up the volume on 8 Mile, take a deep breath, and dig in.

We assume relaxing should feel restful, but the sensation of letting go of tension is the same whether you're relaxing into sleep, into a chest freezer of ice cubes, or violent food poisoning.

HOW TO GRIEVE

Originally published November 2023

Two years ago, my best friend was diagnosed with Stage 3 breast cancer. Two months ago, I went through a breakup. Whether personally or globally, challenges arise.

- Someone you love dies.
- A friend lets you down.
- You're forced to confront your own aging or an aging parent.

Grief is complicated. We aren't taught much about it or how to deal with it.

It is important to take time to mourn a loss.

Here are some habits and practices that might help.

The Role Of Emotions

Sometimes emotions are almost too much to handle. You'll criticize yourself, or other people. You are less happy or healthy than you want to be. But, it turns out, without emotions, we are unable to function in the world.

There are some interesting studies done on the role of emotions. When someone suffers brain damage such that they can't experience emotion, they are also unable to make decisions.

While you sometimes might prefer to do without emotions, the alternative is much worse. You can't enjoy the beautiful things in life if you don't also experience some of the challenges.

Habit: When you are grieving, find something in the same situation, however small, to be grateful for.

Take Time To Grieve

Grief sneaks up at random times. When you least expect it, you may see something that reminds you of someone who's died and the upswell of emotion can be hard to handle.

It doesn't have to be an actual death, either. The loss of a relationship, or even a missed opportunity can be something we need to grieve.

It helps to take time to grieve. Difficult emotions will still come up, but setting aside time does help.

Habit: During a difficult time, carve out at least one minute a day to be present to your emotions. I like to set an alarm on my phone as my cue. I prefer to write during this pause, but any reflective activity can help.

Don't Judge Your Process

Everyone's process for getting over a challenging situation is different. It might mean going to therapy or bitching to a friend. I process emotions by waking up at 5 a.m. full of adrenaline and going for a hard run.

The key is not to judge yourself for the fact that you are grieving. Otherwise, you're not only feeling bad, but you are beating yourself up about it, too.

Don't judge your process.

Habit: Recognize what helps you. Take 10 minutes and write down a list of things that help you take care of yourself.

Grief Takes The Time That It Takes

I was in a serious car accident last year. I knew that it would take some time to heal and I was gentle with myself for the first couple of weeks.

But a few weeks in, I started getting anxious to get back to my movement practice and the rest of my life. I wasn't in pain, but I was still very shaken up and the added pressure didn't help.

In all, it took more than six months to get back to baseline.

Just like healing from physical injury, grief can't be rushed. Healing happens on its own time.

Habit: If you find yourself pressuring yourself to "get over it," decide on a timeline. Give yourself one day, one week, or one month where you won't pressure yourself to "be there" already.

Don't Use Force

The Morningstar Company, which I wrote about in my book Responsive: What It Takes To Create A Thriving Organization, is one of the largest tomato manufacturers in the world. What makes the company unique is that it is self-managed by the employees.

One of the company's two core tenets is "Don't use force" in working with each other.

We're accustomed to using anger, pressure, and blame at work – but at what cost? To the detriment of relationships, our own health, and building the habit of doing more in the future.

Instead of trying to force yourself to feel better, acknowledge your grief. Take time to feel what you are feeling.

Habit: You wouldn't use force – physically or emotionally – with a young child or in an intimate moment with a partner. Treat yourself that same way, even if only for a moment.

We don't get to control what happens to us or to the people we love.

(I can't. If you've figured out how – please email me!)

But we do get to control how we respond.

Grief is a natural part of life. It is how we make sense of what's happened and move forward.

When you're going through a challenge, take the time to acknowledge your grief. I hope some of these habits help.

8

RELATIONSHIPS

HOW TO DATE

*Originally published
February 2026*

I'm happily engaged. I think we might get married next month? But I sat down with a friend recently who is dating – and in San Francisco, no less.

Our meeting was ostensibly a business lunch but quickly turned into a "But how are you doing personally?" conversation. The answer: her dating life was difficult.

My friend is an ambitious professional. She's attractive, smart, and knows what she wants. Yet, over lunch, she shared a multitude of stories about getting ghosted, men pursuing one-night stands, and general frustration.

I didn't have any answers, of course. I can't solve her situation. It has been over a year since going on what I hope to be my last first date – and 20 years since I started dating. I've been on over 1,000 first dates, so I do have some experience.

The Biggest Turn-Off

The most under-addressed aspect of dating is neediness. When you're going on a first date, or even a fifth, neediness is the kiss of death. To illustrate it, I'll share the story of the first time I was fired from a job.

One of my first jobs out of college was as a personal trainer in San Francisco. Gyms are a sales-heavy environment. In order to be in the business, you have to sell clients.

My job entailed teaching a step aerobics class at 5:00 a.m. and then spending the rest of the day walking the gym floor trying to persuade members to hire me. I lasted a week.

On Thursday, my manager sat me down and said if I did not close any new clients by Friday, I'd be fired. I tried my best. And I'm sure I came across as extremely needy. Who doesn't love a personal trainer with the vibe, "Hire me, or I'll get fired tomorrow!"

There's no better way to not go on dates than to really need to go on dates. It is simple: don't approach people or try to date if you feel needy. Fix your attitude first.

13 Dates in 3 Days

In my mid-20s, I was living in a house with several roommates in San Francisco. My roommate, who was at the time engaged, had seen me through several short-term relationships. He had observed the same pattern: I would meet somebody, go on a date, fall into bed with them, and then spend the next three months in a relationship.

He challenged me to go on three first dates with three different people, before going on the second date with any of them. He wanted me to increase my volume.

To make things interesting, we set some stakes. If he won – if I was not able to go on three first dates with three different people – then I would make him and his fiancée a homemade multi-course meal. If I won, he would make me and my date an elaborate meal. It helped that he was a gourmet chef.

I went on a few first dates over the following month, but none that merited a second. Then, one Thursday night, another roommate introduced me to someone, and we immediately hit it off. We made plans to go on a date on a Sunday. But she was visiting my roommate on Friday, and we ended up spending time together. (As I recall, we spent the evening clambering around a public jungle gym?) There was a kiss at the end of that evening, so it was definitely a first date.

And we still had plans to go to lunch on Sunday! This meant I needed to go on at least two more dates on Saturday or Sunday morning before our scheduled lunch to win the bet!

I did everything conceivable to win. At the time, the only dating apps available were OkCupid and Match.com. The following day, I messaged perhaps a hundred people. I called a dozen friends and asked them who they knew. I met somebody in a burrito shop and asked if she'd like to go for a walk.

I ended up going on 13 dates from Saturday morning until Sunday noon. (Or 14 if you count going on a date with a couple – I didn't realize that they would both be there until I showed up for coffee.)

In the end, I won the bet. And I learned that when I was sufficiently motivated, I could generate a lot of dates in a very short period of time.

Where To Date

Bars – One of the few things that I have never done is pick up women in bars. I know it's an environment where people meet, but even before I stopped drinking alcohol, it was never the kind of environment that I particularly enjoyed. My view? Bars are overrated.

Coffee Shops – Long before I owned a coffee shop, I was prone to starting up conversations with people in cafes. Coffee shops offer a great third space – not work, not home – to meet people.

Speed Dating – I've been to a couple of speed dating events. Like all events, it really matters how well it's organized. Most speed dating events aren't very well run, but if you can find one that is, with an appropriate gender balance, it can work.

Niche Hobbies – I'll talk later about being your weird self while dating. For now, though, I think one of the most useful ways to meet somebody is doing things that you love to do and that are very niche. My dear friend Marie met her husband at Gamba Camp!

Organized Co-ed Sports – Organized co-ed sports are a great way to meet people: kickball leagues, running clubs, etc. You're not there to date; you're there to play a game or exercise. But the quality of people is likely higher and they often go out for drinks afterwards.

Non-organized Sports – Another great place to meet people is in environments where everyone is practicing a shared skill outside of an organized setting. Indoor climbing gyms are excellent. Pickup basketball games, etc. These require more willingness to introduce yourself to strangers, but the payoff is worth it.

Social Dancing – The most effective environment I have found for going on dates is social dancing – Argentine tango, Salsa, West Coast Swing, etc. Social dancing provides a functional environment where you can meet and be close to a lot of people in a short period of time. You see them in a vulnerable place, trying to learn something new, being awkward and funny together, and getting a more unfiltered view into who that person is.

Ask Everyone for Help

One of the most ridiculous things that I did in my years-long effort to find a partner was ask everybody I knew to make introductions.

Over the course of three or four months, I reached out to a few dozen professional colleagues – people I only knew as speakers on stage at Responsive Conference or clients of Zander Media – and asked them to make personal introductions.

My only qualifications were that they were people I admired, and I was intimidated to ask them for help.

I told them:

- I'm a 30-something guy.
- I'm a successful bootstrapped entrepreneur.
- I'm looking for a life partner.
- I'm willing to travel anywhere in the world for a first date.
- Would you be willing to make three to five introductions to eligible women that you think I would connect with?

It was incredibly intimidating. But everybody that I talked to was supportive and agreed to help.

Increasing Your Luck Surface Area

One of my favorite phrases is "Increase your luck surface area." The underlying message is that you get lucky through hard work. Of course, luck matters a great deal. I was born a white man in America, after all! But in dating and in life, creating the conditions where you are likely to get lucky makes a great deal of difference.

In the case of dating, that means that you're more likely to meet people when you are going out several nights a week than if you're staying at home. You're more likely to meet clients when you go to business conferences. You're more likely to land a new job if you ask current and former professional colleagues for introductions.

All of these things take hard work. Put yourself in the condition where you are more likely to be successful – and you will be.

Dating Apps Are Slot Machines

I met my fiancée on Bumble. Almost certainly, I'd never have met her otherwise. But dating apps aren't designed to get you a date. They're designed to keep you on the screen.

Dating apps are incentivized to keep you on the app–that's their business model.

Treat the apps with discipline – spend an allotted amount of time on the apps each day – just like you would going to the gym or brushing your teeth. Treat using dating apps as a tool, not a distraction.

Set aside specific times to match and to message – Don't let yourself doom scroll on dating apps. Instead, set aside a few minutes or even an hour each day to match with people and message with them.

Get off the apps – The thing that dating apps can do is connect you with people you might not otherwise have met. Now that you've met them, get off the app! As soon as possible, take that digital conversation to text, a phone call, or in real life.

Communicate like a human – There are a lot of scammers and people wasting time. If you get a bad vibe off somebody, move on quickly.

Most People Are Flaky

Being reliable – simply doing what you say you're going to do – is a big advantage. Because, unfortunately, most people are flaky.

This is triply true in dating where inherent flakiness is combined with all sorts of hang-ups, unprocessed trauma, and a lack of clarity as to what someone actually wants.

It's just a sad fact that you're going to have to wade through a lot of unreliable people to find some diamonds in the rough.

Get Ahead By Being Yourself

The single biggest thing that you can do to increase your odds of a good match is to be true to who you actually are.

I like phone calls. And so, what my fiancée and I have come to call "date 0" was a two-hour phone call. We covered a lot of ground in that first conversation that might not otherwise have been things that people talk about on a first date. On our actual first date – which happened the next day – we shared intimate details about our families and past relationships.

Of course you want to present a polished version of yourself. I washed my car before meeting my fiancée for the first time in case she wanted me to drop her off at her front door at the end of the night. But you also have to be yourself, so that you don't get found out later for having lied about who you really are.

The Goal Should Be Connection

Most of us early in our dating lives are trying to get something – to get laid, to find love, whatever it is. And when we approach dating from that place of need, it rarely works.

If all you're trying to do is assess whether this person is a good long-term romantic match, you're in for a long road.

Your goal should be to connect with the person you're talking to, first. And then let everything else happen from there.

Dating is Selling

Everything that I've ever talked about selling applies to dating too.

Know Yourself

If you don't know what you're looking for, you're much less likely to find it. Unfortunately, in order to know what you're looking for, you have to know yourself. Self-knowledge in dating – or choosing any kind of partner – is the ultimate competitive advantage.

Tell Compelling Stories

I talked extensively about storytelling and how to tell your own story so simply and effectively. Telling stories about yourself that are real, compelling, authentic, and vulnerable will go a long way to connecting on a first date.

Play More

My fiancée finds me hilarious and I'm never quite sure why. But I have learned that when I am most authentically myself – the silliest, most playful version of myself – I can be quite compelling. Don't try to force humor, but when you're playful you're more likely to connect with others.

Ask Sincere Questions

I asked my fiancée all sorts of vulnerable questions on our first phone call and first in-person date. I caveated them with "please don't feel obliged to answer, and I was wondering…". But I did ask. Ask the questions that you're sincerely curious about, and they get to the heart of who the other person is.

Be Flexible with the Outcome

One of the 13 dates I went on was with somebody who stated very quickly that she wasn't in a good place to date. But she offered that if I'd like to, we could still get together over coffee.

We ended up climbing trees in San Francisco's Golden Gate Park, sitting in the tops of trees and sharing book recommendations.

I don't remember her name, but I do recall the unexpected delight that this "non-date" turned into a sincere friendship.

When you're flexible with the outcome, you can often get more than you expected.

Prioritize Yourself

Don't burn yourself out trying to date. It's tempting to hope that just the next minute, the next match, or the next first date will land you the relationship that you want. It probably won't.

If you don't prioritize yourself over your dating prospects, you likely won't get very many dates, and you certainly won't match with somebody who's actually a good fit.

HOW TO ASK FOR WHAT YOU WANT

Originally published December 2023

I'm traveling in Mexico with my family this week. It is really special: the first time in decades that my family has traveled internationally together and the first time we're doing so with my two nephews. And operating in such close proximity reveals some habits that I don't love.

We don't use the word "please," for example. Growing up, please was mostly used as a demand in moments of peak frustration. "Will you please do what I asked!" More generally, we (and I am very much included in this assessment) are not very good at asking directly for what we want.

Except for pushy telemarketers, most of us don't ask for things directly. And almost nobody asks without some amount of demand or expectation.

But asking is really important – whether in closing a sale or voicing an opinion. Without a clear expression of what you want, it's hard to get anywhere quickly.

Here are some habits that I'm practicing with my family – and will be exploring in more depth in a workshop on selling I'm planning for the New Year.

Recognize What You Want

It is pretty hard to ask clearly for something that you aren't clear about wanting, yourself.

Identify what you want. If you don't know, write a list of things you might want and pick the ones that seem the best.

Know Why

After you've recognized what you want, consider why. For a primer on finding your why, check out last week's article on the topic.

Brainstorm a list of reasons why. Choose several! The more reasons, the stronger your desire will be.

Let Fear Be a Guide

Fear is an excellent guide. When you're afraid of selling your idea, your product, or voicing your opinion, that's a great reason to move towards that fear, not away from it.

Start Small

Starting small is a secret to unlocking any sort of behavior change.

Don't compare yourself to anyone else's ability to persuade, ask or close a deal. Just take the next small step from where you are currently.

Practice In Advance

Asking for what you want requires rehearsal, just like athletic performance and everything else in life.

If you aren't good at selling your idea, that's probably because you haven't practiced!

Start by writing out your pitch. I suggest writing out a pitch in three formats – one sentence, one paragraph, and one page.

Iterate As You Go

Great salespeople – greats in any domain – don't just get good at their thing and then stop progressing. They continue to iterate.

Learn from every pitch, notice what works and iterate as you go.

Ask For What You Want

Ask for what you want!

When you are talking to someone, writing to someone, speaking to them on the phone, or promoting your thing on social media, end with a clear ask.

- "Would you like to buy?"
- "Would you like to go to dinner?"
- "Do you agree with my opinion?"

Get Feedback

A day or a week after you've tried to sell someone or pitch your idea, ask them about their experience. How was it received? Is there anything they think you could have done better?

There's a lot about my family that I'm grateful for. And we come with quirks and challenges.

I'm not proud of the extent to which I don't comfortably use the word "please" and hesitate to make my opinion known. But when I see those dynamics within the broader context of my family, I have a bit more empathy and understanding.

The only way to get better at asking for what you want is by observing where you are now and taking the next steps from there.

HOW TO SET BOUNDARIES

*Originally published
July 2025*

A few years ago, a friend and I kept trying to make plans. I canceled several times – once due to a car crash – and after the third or fourth reschedule, she told me it wasn't working for her and that she was going to deprioritize our friendship. I apologized, we talked it through, and agreed I'd take responsibility for reaching out.

I followed up for six months with no response. Eventually, she let me know she was no longer interested in being friends.

I was hurt. We'd had a clear agreement, and she'd gone back on it. That experience stuck with me – and led me to adopt my best friend's "Free Pass System."

When you notice someone does something that doesn't work for you, you are responsible for telling them so. The key is to tell the other person before the issue has become insurmountable.

Tell the person that their behavior won't work for you going forward, and why. Detail the specifics of what you want to change going forward.

They get a Free Pass up until this point – assuming you still want a relationship with this person. Grant them grace up until this point. That's only reasonable because you haven't told them that their behavior doesn't work for you!

But you have to set clear consequences. Setting consequences is hard because most of us don't have practice. First, articulate the boundaries for yourself. Then, describe them to the other person.

Consequences aren't punishment – they're about clarity. They tell the other person what you will do if the behavior continues, so that you're not reacting or building resentment, but fostering the relationship that you want.

Here are a few examples:

- If someone is flaky after you've communicated that it doesn't work for you, don't schedule with them again.
- If someone shares a secret that you shared in confidence, don't share private information with them in the future.

- If a client doesn't pay on time, add delinquency fees to the bill.
- Boundaries can be small and nuanced – like the fact I don't talk to my parents if they sound crabby at the start of a phone call because that's when our conversations are most likely to go poorly.

To summarize the Free Pass System:

- When someone crosses a boundary, identify the boundary to yourself, and then to the other person.
- If you don't want them in your life anymore, cut them out of your life.
- Otherwise, give them grace – a Free Pass – up until now.
- Describe to them the clear consequences if they do the unwanted behavior again.
- Then, if they exhibit the behavior again, enact the consequences you've communicated.

I don't bemoan the loss of friendship with the person who wrote me off. As a result, I learned how to set better boundaries. Whether in friendships, family, or business, the Free Pass System helps you set and hold boundaries. It won't fix every relationship, but it will improve the ones worth keeping.

HOW TO HELP PEOPLE DO WHAT THEY WANT

Originally published December 2023

My family read together each night throughout my childhood. We'd sit on our faded blue living room couch and listen to my father read aloud.

One of the books we discovered together was My Family and Other Animals by famed naturalist Gerald Durrell. Gerald related stories from living on the Green island of Corfu with his fractious siblings and widowed mother between 1935 and 1939 – and the beginning of his naturalist adventures.

One story stands out in my memory. Gerald, a precocious 10 year old, asked for birthday presents. Very carefully, from each family member he requested a gift which that family member is well suited to giving.

From his brother Larry (who became the author Lawrence Durrell), Gerald requested a pair of binoculars because he knew his intellectual brother appreciated the importance of observation and detail. Gerald's brother Leslie was the most practical member of the family, so Gerald requested a sensible ersatz alpine hat.

I've always been impressed with the poise and forethought Gerald showed in assessing the personality of each person and requesting an appropriate gift.

As I'm traveling in Mexico this week with my own family, that forethought seems even more useful. It is hard to play to the strengths of another person, but worth the effort.

Help People To Do Things

Years ago, my old professor BJ Fogg advised me that the best way to help people was to enable them to do things that they already wanted to do.

You are going to be more successful if the idea you are selling is one the other person is already inclined to believe.

Develop The Empathy To Know What They Want

Gerald Durrell accurately assessed the strengths of each member of his family. To do so required a lot of empathy, an understanding of each person.

Practice this kind of empathy through curiosity. As I discussed in my article "Everything is Sales," selling is rooted in discovery and a deep curiosity about your customer.

In order to sell, you must first develop the curiosity to understand who the other person is and what they need.

Spend Time With People Doing Their Thing

My good friend David and I live 30 minutes apart and would enjoy seeing each other more than we do. But we only get together only a few times a year.

We share a love of weight lifting and recently went to the gym together for the first time. Now we're scheduled to spend time weight lifting together once a month.

Identify the person or group that you want to spend time with. Adopt their activity or find something that you both enjoy that you can do together.

I Only Go on Dates That I'd Be Happy to Do Solo

First dates have a low probability of success, whether due to cancelation or a lack of chemistry. Years ago, back at the dawn of online dating, I decided to only go on first dates that I would be equally happy to do solo.

Prioritize things that you'll enjoy, even if the company or outcome is uncertain.

Maintain Flexible Goals

In my early 20s, I built a company helping kids with autism and their families.

With children with autism, progress is often so gradual that most people wouldn't notice any change. And because progress can be so unpredictable, it helps to maintain flexible goals.

The more you cling to a specific outcome, the less likely it is to happen!

In selling, too, not getting attached to a specific outcome results in better learning and more growth.

Gerald Durrell took enormous delight in carefully requesting the exact thing of each family member that they would be most inclined to give him.

Even if the rest of us aren't quite so meticulous, there are some lessons to be learned about selling and persuasion from his example.

HOW TO TRAVEL WITH FAMILY

Originally published December 2023

I'm traveling with my family to Mexico for two weeks this winter. The trip is a throwback to holidays from my childhood. Every other year, my family avoided the holidays altogether and traveled to Latin America. As a kid, I was sad to miss the holidays, but in retrospect those international trips were formative. This will be the first family trip in a decade and the first time with my nephews (7 and 10).

Know Why

When I took a month-long trip with my mother to Ghana, I had to get very clear in the months leading up to the trip why I was going. And my purpose for taking the trip wasn't to have a great experience.

Visiting Ghana was a lifelong dream of my mother's and a trip she wouldn't have attempted alone. My primary reason for going to Africa was to support her; to facilitate her having a positive experience.

As you are heading into an experience with family, ask yourself why you are prioritizing spending time in this way:

What Are You Hoping To Get Out Of It?

What do you want for your family members?

The more clearly you know why, the better you will be at boundaries and making productive use of the time.

Habit: Write down 10 different reasons "why" you are taking the action that you are. They won't all feel true, but you'll find something new through the exercise.

There's No Problem So Big You Can't Walk Away

I use this phrase, which is oft repeated by a close friend, to remind myself that I have agency. We always have the ability to leave – even when it feels like we don't.

It is something of a cardinal sin in my family to leave a conversation or issue unresolved. And yet I'm always calmer for stepping away for ten minutes and coming back to the issue later.

Any of us is free to take a break or walk away at any time.

Habit: Remind yourself, maybe even aloud, that "There's no problem so big I can't walk away." Repeating that serves as a reminder that you are not stuck in a difficult situation.

Take A Pee Break

Years ago, a friend taught me the trick of taking a "pee break." Maybe you actually need to use the toilet, but that's beside the point.

The goal is that when you are upset you take a couple of minutes to reorient yourself and come back refreshed.

Under very few circumstances is it considered socially inappropriate to take a couple of minutes out of a conversation "because I have to use the restroom." And often you come back better able to handle whatever challenge has been going on.

Habit: Practice "taking a pee break" when the stakes are low. During an otherwise unheated conversation say, "I'll be back in 2 minutes. I need to use the restroom." The better you get at taking a break, the better you'll be able to when things get heated.

Therapy With Family

I'm a proponent of facilitated conversation: therapy, coaching or anything else that works for you.

In advance of our trip to Ghana, my mother and I went to therapy together. The objective was to create some guidelines about what we might expect while we were traveling in Africa, and how to collaborate better.

My mother and I walked out of therapy with a new willingness to listen to each other, which led to a gentler trip in Ghana than might have happened otherwise. (It was still an intense experience!)

Habit: Organize a facilitated conversation. It might not change anything, but it might also result in less drama.

Family Meetings

We had regular family meetings growing up. Once every few weeks, our family of four would sit down and discuss challenges that had come up recently.

I don't remember what got discussed, but "let's have a family meeting" remains my family's shorthand when communication is getting tough.

Habit: Schedule a brief "family meeting." The goal isn't to change anybody's behavior, but to create space for airing of grievances – so they don't bubble over at inopportune times.

As I get ready to spend two weeks in close quarters with my family in Mexico, I know that I am going to need to practice a lot of these habits and tools. I hope that one of these habits is useful for you as you head into your own holiday plans.

HOW TO CHANGE SOMEONE YOU LOVE

Originally published July 2023

Last month, I went for a hike to celebrate my father's 74th birthday. My father is a botanist, and it was with profound joy that I watched him meticulously bend over to identify flowers amidst the California bloom. Aside from being happy to see my father doing something he loved, I was moved because this simple habit, walking and bending down, was almost impossible for him 5 short years ago.

For most of the last two decades, my father suffered chronic back pain – the result of years of pounding concrete as a runner.

It pained me to see him suffer and I desperately wanted to help him. I tried everything I could think of to get him to change his habits and improve his back pain.

Nothing I did had a lasting impact. Hard as I might try, I couldn't "fix" him and my father would inevitably return to the habits that caused pain in the first place. Moreover, my judgments and pressure created a wedge between us.

Then, after decades of worsening pain, my father underwent back surgery, which resolved the back pain.

Early in his recovery, I lent him my Concept 2 Rower and a few free weights. I'd recently taken up rowing, and built out a home gym. While I had no expectation that he'd adopt a new physical routine, I enthusiastically shared what I'd been learning. I taught him a few simple exercises: how to row with good form, how to lift some basic weights, and how to hang from a bar.

When I came back to reclaim my Concept 2 Rower a month later, he was rowing and practicing the exercises I taught him every day. In the two years since, I've helped him continue to build on his exercise habits until he's exercising for two hours most days!

My father's transformation has been profound. He is out of pain, working in his garden, and exercising several hours a day. I am immensely proud, but ultimately can't take much credit for his recovery.

They Have To Want It

I have some tough news: you can't change people. People have to want change in order to make progress.

If they don't want to change their behavior, that's where to begin. You can start with data, with a personal appeal, or any other approach that you think will work to help them want to change. But without the core desire - their "why" - change is impossible.

Let Go Of The Outcome

My biggest learning, and one that I've had to confront again and again, is that in order to help someone we love, we have to let go of the need for them to change. You have to let go of the outcome.

You don't have to care less, but we all know when we're being pressured, even if it isn't explicit. And - I don't know about you - but when I'm pressured, I dig in my heels and resist change all the more!

To encourage someone you love to change their behavior, you have to first get comfortable with the fact that they may not ever change.

Attitude Is Everything

I spent many years helping kids with autism build better habits and learned an invaluable lesson: attitude trumps everything.

Many of the kids I worked with were non-verbal, and they, and their families, would often be bossed around by therapists and specialists who believed things should only be done a certain way.

These kids learned to respond, primarily, to a caregiver's attitude. And I learned that when I showed up with a loving presence, we'd be able to connect much more easily.

This same approach holds true for everyone. To help someone you love change, showing up with a kind and gentle attitude is more than half the battle.

Be Like Gravity

The best invitations feel like gravity; impossible to resist

We've all been sold to by pushy salespeople. Gravity is the opposite.

Instead of pushing and pressuring, be so engaging, so inviting, that people want to gravitate towards you, and towards the changes you're asking for.

Start Where They Are

For someone to change, you have to begin with where they are right now.

That's true for any of us in pursuing any kind of behavior change. And it is particularly true when you're wanting someone else to make progress.

We can't run a marathon tomorrow if today we're healing a sprained ankle. We can only build small habits from where we are right now.

Change Takes The Time That It Takes

This comes back, full circle, to "we can't control people."

Change takes time, usually more than we want to give it. This is as true of change in others as it is for change within ourselves!

Helping someone we love takes the time that it takes. We can't dictate how long a transformation will take. Impatience can not only create a negative atmosphere of pressure that slows down progress, but it also can mean that we miss important markers of progress along the way or lose the opportunity to be part of someone's journey as they come back from a setback.

During an interview with author and conflict resolution specialist Dana Caspersen, she said to me: "Not only can you not change people, but it is none of your damned business."

My judgment of the habits that led to my father's injury and my pressure for him to change did not help him recover, but actually got in the way of us having a healthy relationship.

Trying to get anyone to do something that they don't already want to do is wasted effort. All that we can do is support and celebrate where someone is, and encourage them to take incrementally small steps in the direction we'll hope they'll go.

Closing Thoughts

Thank You

Before you go, I'd like to thank you for reading *This Might Work*.

If any of these stories and tools have been useful to you, I'd like to hear about it! Email me at robin@zandermedia.com.

Would You Like To Know More?

If you've liked this book, you'll enjoy Snafu, my weekly newsletter about persuasion, influence, sales, and navigating our chaotic world.

It's free and comes out each week. Visit www.robinpzander.com to subscribe.

More Books by Robin

I have published two other books that you might enjoy.

How to Do a Handstand: Learn to Master a Fearless Handstand in 20 Days or Less

Responsive: What It Takes To Create A Thriving Organization

Made in the USA
Coppell, TX
27 February 2026